National Trust
Favourite Recipes

National Trust
Favourite Recipes

Clive Goudercourt
& Rebecca Janaway

First published in the United Kingdom in 2022 by
National Trust Books
43 Great Ormond Street
London WC1N 3HZ

Copyright © National Trust, 2022
Recipe development by Clive Goudercourt
    and Rebecca Janaway
Edited and compiled by Maggie Ramsay
The moral rights of the authors have
been asserted.

ISBN 9781911657446

A CIP catalogue record for this book is available
from the British Library.

30 29 28 27 26 25 24 23 22
10 9 8 7 6 5 4 3 2 1

Reproduction by Rival Colour Ltd, UK
Printed and bound by Toppan Leefung Ltd, China

This book is available at National Trust shops
and online at www.nationaltrustbooks.co.uk

MIX
Paper from
responsible sources
FSC® C104723
www.fsc.org

Contents

Introduction 6

Soups 12

Salads 30

Light Meals 46

One-pots and Mains 72

Desserts 104

Cakes and Bakes 124

Index 156

Introduction

A visit to a National Trust property promises fascinating history, awe-inspiring natural beauty, and a truly memorable setting for quality time with family and friends. And for many visitors, no National Trust experience is complete without a stop at the café – whether for a fortifying pre-walk lunch, or the chance to reflect upon a well-spent day over tea and cake. As Development Chefs, we are always looking for ways to make that experience the best it can possibly be. We're passionate about food, and we want to do more than feed our visitors: we want to inspire them.

That's why we've compiled this latest collection of gems from our culinary repertoire: *National Trust Favourite Recipes* is an invitation for you to share with us in the joy of food. Its goal is to enable you to cook up some of our most delectable dishes, enjoy them from the comfort of your own home, and share them with your loved ones. Take a little bit of the National Trust home with you, and evoke fond memories as you fill your kitchen with the mouth-watering aroma of freshly-baked pastry, or awaken your taste buds with the zing of a refreshing salad.

Seasonality is a real priority for us. Our kitchen teams often use herbs, vegetables and fruit from our kitchen gardens and orchards – and you can't get fresher than that! Produce also comes from the Trust's tenant farmers, who are working hard to protect the countryside, as well as from other local and regional suppliers. Working in this way means that the food on offer in our cafés changes throughout the year. Sourcing locally allows us to support local communities as well as helping us to ensure that the food we sell is produced sustainably and meets animal-welfare standards. Even when we must look further afield for ingredients, we choose our suppliers with care, seeking out foods that are produced ethically and in an environmentally conscious way. The profit generated

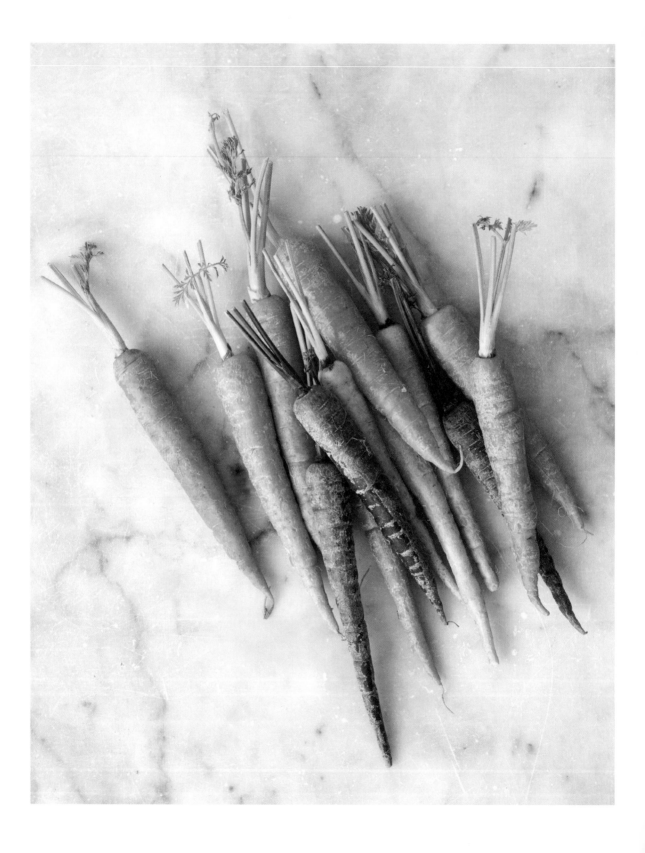

by our cafés then helps to look after the places in the National Trust's care, so we take pride in producing good food that does good.

This book includes year-round recipe inspiration to help you make the most of gluts of home-grown fruit and veg, as well as foraged ingredients and lucky finds at your local farmers' market. In spring, the dayglo-pink sticks of 'forced' rhubarb make a spectacular baked cheesecake (page 108), while the leaves of wild garlic, with their unmistakable fragrance, are the main ingredient of our super-simple wild garlic soup (page 14). You may not be short of ideas for summer's bountiful fruit and vegetables, but have you explored the full array of aromatic herbs and flowers available? For something special, try our lavender shortbread (page 137) or lavender and honey panna cotta (page 113). Embrace the colder months with a brisk walk on a frosty day; you'll be warmed by the thought of a beef cobbler (page 102) waiting for you to tuck into when you get home. Soups are guaranteed comfort food, too: they're as nourishing for the soul as they are packed with nutritious ingredients. Heartening when it's cold outside and invigorating in warmer weather, the vibrant colours of Tuscan-style tomato soup (page 19) or golden cauliflower, turmeric and coconut soup (page 27) will brighten any day.

We're committed to serving trusted classics alongside new and intriguing flavours, to ensure we're providing all our visitors with an experience that will delight them and exceed their expectations. Among the most enjoyable aspects of our job is keeping an eye on the latest food trends from around the world, creating new dishes and subtly adapting stalwarts of the menu. A traditional cream tea is an enduringly popular choice at National Trust cafés – even with the difficulties of the past few years, we've served up well over a million fruit scones every year. But a few years ago, the chefs at the Dunwich Heath tea-room had a flash of genius: they fused an American favourite with a British one and came up with the gently spiced pumpkin pie scone (page 145). Another one of our best-loved teatime treats is the Victoria sponge. We've recently given this classic an exciting upgrade with the help of lemon curd, orange zest and a drizzle of orange syrup: on page 139 you can find out how to make your own delicious and uplifting orange and lemon cake.

You may have noticed a wider range of vegetarian and vegan choices in our cafés and tea-rooms, as well as dishes made from ingredients not containing gluten. We want to give more people the chance to enjoy our recipes, so besides the many sweet and savoury fruit- and veg-based dishes on offer, we've been developing enticing treats such as gluten-free beetroot, kale and Brie quiche (page 65), a fabulously simple yet rich vegan chocolate fudge cake (page 133), and one of Clive's latest triumphs: a vegan chilli non carne (page 95) that packs an amazing punch of flavour.

Join us as we celebrate some of the most delicious dishes that have appeared in National Trust cafés and tea-rooms in recent years. We'll take a fresh look at old favourites, lending a new twist to the flavour here or introducing a more health-conscious ingredient there. We hope this collection of recipes will inspire you to discover some new favourites of your own.

Clive and Rebecca
Development Chefs, National Trust

Soups

Wild garlic soup

Wild garlic flourishes in moist woodlands in springtime. Abundant in supply and recognisable by their distinctive, savoury aroma, the tender young leaves give this soup its vivid green colour.

Vegetarian | Serves: 4 | Prep: 15 minutes | Cook: 30 minutes

20g (¾oz) butter

1 large onion, thinly sliced

1 medium–large potato, peeled and chopped

1 litre (1¾ pints) vegetable stock

3–4 good handfuls, about 100g (3½oz), wild garlic leaves and stems, washed

2 tbsp crème fraîche

Salt and pepper

Melt the butter in a large saucepan over a low heat. Add the onion and cook for 8–10 minutes, stirring from time to time, until softened.

Add the potato to the pan along with the stock. Turn up the heat and bring to the boil, then cover and simmer for 15–20 minutes until the potato is cooked.

Remove from the heat and add the wild garlic. Purée the soup in the pan using a stick blender, or transfer to a blender and blend until smooth.

Season to taste, then ladle into bowls and finish with a dollop of crème fraîche.

COOK'S TIPS

It's illegal to dig up wild roots unless you have the landowner's permission, so if you are foraging fresh wild garlic, only pick the leaves. Pick away from paths and roads.

Positive identification is important, as wild garlic leaves can be confused with some seriously poisonous plants. Wild garlic smells powerfully garlicky when crushed in your fingers.

To use, gently rinse in cold water and pat dry.

Onion soup

A hearty French bistro dish that's practically a meal in itself. It's usually topped with a slice or two of bread and grilled cheese, but in this case, we replace the bread with gluten-free cheese scones.

Gluten-free, vegetarian | Serves: 4 | Prep: 15 minutes | Cook: 1 hour

30g (1oz) butter

1 tbsp vegetable oil

1kg (2lb 3oz) onions, finely sliced

2 tsp caster sugar

5 garlic cloves, thinly sliced

2–3 sprigs of sage, leaves finely chopped, or 1 tsp dried sage

200ml (7fl oz) dry white wine

600ml (1 pint) vegetable stock

2 gluten-free cheese scones (see Cook's Tips)

70g (2½oz) vegetarian Cheddar cheese, grated

Salt and pepper

Put the butter and oil in a large saucepan over a medium heat. When the butter has melted, add the onions, stir well and fry for about 10 minutes until lightly coloured.

Add the sugar, cover with a lid or some foil and fry for 20–30 minutes, stirring occasionally.

Add the garlic and sage and fry for a further 5–6 minutes. Add the wine, stock and salt and pepper to taste. Bring to the boil, then reduce the heat and simmer for about 10 minutes.

Preheat the grill. Slice the scones in half, top with the grated cheese and grill until the cheese melts and begins to brown.

Taste the soup and adjust the seasoning, then ladle into bowls. Carefully slide a toasted scone into each bowl and serve immediately.

If you have heatproof soup bowls, you can serve this the traditional way: float the scone (or slice of baguette) directly on the soup, sprinkle the cheese over the top and place under a hot grill until the cheese melts and begins to brown.

COOK'S TIPS

To make this recipe gluten-free, use gluten-free scones (see page 49 and omit the bacon and chives from them if you wish). If gluten is not an issue, you can use slices of baguette instead.

Thai-style green curry soup

A taste of Thailand in a bowl. Make the most of vegetables picked from your garden or left over from another dish. If you don't have one of the vegetables listed here, just use more of another variety.

Vegan | Serves: 4 | **Prep: 20 minutes** | **Cook: 20 minutes**

1 tbsp vegetable oil

5 spring onions, thinly sliced

55g (2oz) Thai green curry paste (see Cook's Tip)

850ml (1½ pints) hot vegetable stock

70g (2½oz) leeks, cut into strips

70g (2½oz) fresh or frozen spinach

70g (2½oz) green cabbage, finely shredded

30g (1oz) mangetout, sliced

1 garlic clove, finely chopped

120ml (4fl oz) coconut milk

100g (3½oz) dried fine rice noodles (vermicelli)

A small handful of fresh coriander, chopped

Grated zest and juice of ½–1 lime

Salt and pepper

Heat the oil in a large saucepan over a medium heat, add the spring onions and fry for 1 minute, stirring from time to time, until softened. Add the Thai curry paste, stir well and cook for a couple of minutes. Add the hot stock, stir well and bring to the boil. Add the vegetables and garlic, then add the coconut milk and continue to simmer.

Meanwhile, cook the rice noodles or soak in boiling water according to the pack instructions (but do not rinse in cold water).

Remove the soup pan from the heat, drain the rice noodles and add them to the soup. Leave to stand for 2 minutes. (Adding the noodles when the pan is off the heat helps to prevent them from breaking down too much.)

Season to taste. Stir in the coriander and the lime zest and juice and ladle into bowls to serve.

COOK'S TIP

Not all Thai green curry paste is vegan, so check the label when you shop.

Tuscan-style tomato soup

This tasty twist on a classic tomato soup, topped with rustic croutons and a swirl of herby pistou oil, makes the most of home-grown tomatoes and fresh herbs. The tomatoes are roasted to intensify their flavour.

Vegan | Serves: 4 | Prep: 30 minutes | Cook: 45 minutes–1 hour

800g (1¾lb) tomatoes

1 tbsp olive oil

1 small onion, chopped

2 garlic cloves, chopped

1 tbsp tomato purée

1 red pepper, deseeded and chopped

700ml (1¼ pints) hot vegetable stock

10g (⅓oz) fresh basil leaves

2 tsp caster sugar

Salt and pepper

Pistou oil

30g (1oz) fresh basil

30g (1oz) fresh parsley

30g (1oz) fresh mint

50g (1¾oz) young spinach

1 garlic clove, roughly chopped

5 tbsp olive oil

Croutons

100g (3½oz) day-old rustic bread, thickly sliced

2 tbsp extra-virgin olive oil or cold-pressed rapeseed oil

Preheat the oven to 190°C/180°C fan/gas 5 and line a roasting tin with non-stick baking paper. Cut the tomatoes in half and if they have hard, woody 'cores', cut these out with a small sharp knife. Place the tomatoes cut-side down in the roasting tin and roast for 15–20 minutes until softened and the skins have lifted away from the flesh. Remove the tomatoes from the oven and leave to cool slightly, then pinch off all the skins, saving any roasting juices.

Meanwhile, make the pistou oil. Remove any tough stalks from the herbs and spinach, then place in a food processor with the garlic and olive oil and some salt and pepper. Blend until fairly smooth. Set aside until ready to serve.

Turn the oven down to 160°C/150°C fan/gas 3.

Place a large saucepan over a medium–high heat, add the oil and the onion and fry for about 5 minutes until starting to soften. Add the garlic and tomato purée and cook for a further 5 minutes, stirring constantly.

Stir in the skinned roasted tomatoes and their roasting juices, the red pepper and the hot stock and bring to the boil. Cover and simmer for 15 minutes until the pepper is tender.

To make the croutons, cut the bread into bite-sized pieces. Spread the pieces in a single layer on a baking sheet, drizzle with the oil and season with salt and pepper. Bake for about 10 minutes, until golden and crisp.

Remove the soup pan from the heat and stir in the basil, sugar, salt and pepper. Purée the soup in the pan using a stick blender, or transfer to a blender and blend until smooth. Taste and adjust the seasoning.

Ladle the soup into bowls and top with croutons and a drizzle of pistou oil.

Courgette, pea and basil soup

Sometimes courgettes seem to grow faster than you can pick them. Luckily, they're very versatile. This light, summery soup is a great way to boost your five-a-day.

Vegan | Serves: 4 | Prep: 10 minutes | Cook: 15–20 minutes

1 tbsp vegetable oil

150g (5½oz) leeks, thinly sliced

500g (1lb 2oz) courgettes, roughly chopped

1 garlic clove, roughly chopped

600ml (1 pint) hot vegetable stock

200g (7oz) fresh podded or frozen peas

15g (½oz) basil, shredded, plus extra to garnish

Grated zest and juice of 1 lemon

Salt and pepper

Heat the oil in a large saucepan over a medium heat. Add the leeks, courgettes and garlic and fry for about 10 minutes, stirring from time to time, until the vegetables are soft and starting to colour.

Add the hot stock and peas to the pan, bring to the boil and boil for 2–3 minutes. Add the basil, lemon zest and juice and bring back to the boil.

Remove from the heat and purée the soup in the pan using a stick blender, or transfer to a blender and blend until smooth.

Season to taste, then ladle into bowls and garnish with basil leaves.

Roasted red pepper soup

Bright, light and fresh, with a hint of smoky seasoning, this vibrant soup is perfect whatever the weather or the season.

Vegan | Serves: 4 | Prep: 15 minutes | Cook: 45 minutes

600g (1lb 5oz) red peppers, halved and deseeded

1½ tbsp olive oil

200g (7oz) red onions, chopped

150g (5½oz) carrots, chopped

1 garlic clove, crushed

1 tsp smoked paprika

600ml (1 pint) hot vegetable stock or water

½ lemon

Salt and pepper

Preheat the oven to 190°C/180°C fan/gas 5 and line a roasting tin with non-stick baking paper.

Put the peppers in the roasting tin and drizzle with half the oil. Roast for about 30 minutes or until soft and beginning to char, with the skins starting to peel off. Remove from the oven, cover the tin tightly with foil and set aside.

Place a large saucepan over a medium heat, add the remaining oil, onions, carrots and garlic and stir well, then cover and cook over a medium–low heat for 10–15 minutes until soft.

Meanwhile, peel off the pepper skins (they should come off easily), holding the peppers over the roasting tin to capture the juices.

Add the smoked paprika and the roasted red peppers and their roasting juices to the saucepan and stir well. Add the hot stock, bring to the boil, then simmer for 3–4 minutes.

Purée the soup in the pan using a stick blender, or transfer to a blender and blend until smooth. Season to taste with salt, pepper and a good squeeze or two of lemon juice.

COOK'S TIPS

Make sure to add the roasting juices from the peppers.

Look out for slightly imperfect 'wonky' peppers, which are fine for this soup.

Wild mushroom and barley soup

In this rich, dark soup, dried mushrooms complement fresh ones to give an intense flavour.
Plump, tender grains of pearl barley make this a really satisfying lunch on an autumn day.

Vegan | Serves: 4 | **Prep: 20 minutes** | **Cook: about 45 minutes–1 hour**

70g (2½oz) pearl barley,
  rinsed
20g (¾oz) dried porcini
  or mixed mushrooms
350ml (12½fl oz) boiling
  water
2 tbsp vegetable oil
1 large onion, finely
  chopped
100g (3½oz) leek, finely
  sliced
2 tbsp fresh thyme leaves
2 garlic cloves, crushed
340g (12oz) mushrooms,
  half roughly chopped,
  half sliced
1 tbsp plain flour
Salt and pepper
2 tbsp fresh chopped
  chives, to garnish

Add the pearl barley to a saucepan of boiling, lightly salted water, bring back
to the boil, then partly cover with a lid and simmer for 30–40 minutes until the
barley is cooked and tender. Drain and set aside.

Meanwhile, put the dried mushrooms in a food processor and blitz to a
powder. Tip into a bowl, pour in 150ml (5fl oz) of the boiling water and
leave to soak.

Heat half the oil in a large saucepan over a medium heat. Add the onion and
leek and fry for about 5 minutes, stirring from time to time, until softened and
lightly coloured.

Stir in the thyme and garlic and season well. Add the chopped mushrooms,
increase the heat, stir briefly, then cook for about 5 minutes until the
mushrooms start to release their liquid. Sprinkle in the flour and stir over the
heat for about 2 minutes. Tip in the dried-mushroom liquid and gradually add
about 200ml (7fl oz) boiling water, stirring all the time to prevent any lumps
from forming as you bring the soup to the boil.

Fry the sliced mushrooms in the remaining oil until lightly coloured; set aside.

Purée the soup in the pan using a stick blender, or transfer to a blender and
blend until smooth. Stir in the fried mushrooms and the cooked barley and
season well. Ladle into bowls and sprinkle with chives.

Spicy carrot and coconut soup

Thai red curry paste adds spicy background warmth to this comforting carrot soup.
It's just the thing to warm you up after a refreshing walk on a chilly day.

Vegan | Serves: 4 | Prep: 20 minutes | Cook: 40 minutes

1 tbsp vegetable oil

1 large onion, roughly
  chopped

2 garlic cloves, roughly
  chopped

2.5cm (1 inch) piece of
  root ginger, peeled
  and chopped

1 tbsp Thai red curry paste
  (see Cook's Tip)

600g (1lb 5oz) carrots,
  roughly chopped

85oml (1½ pints) hot
  vegetable stock

85ml (3fl oz) coconut
  milk, plus extra to
  garnish (optional)

1 lime, halved

Dash of soy sauce (optional)

Salt and pepper

A small handful of fresh
  coriander, chopped, and
  some chilli flakes to
  garnish (optional)

Place a large saucepan over a medium heat, add the oil, onion, garlic and ginger and fry, stirring from time to time, for 8–10 minutes until softened. Add the Thai curry paste and fry for about 3 minutes, stirring frequently to prevent it from sticking.

Add the carrots, stir well, then add the hot stock and bring to the boil. Reduce the heat, cover the pan and cook for about 25 minutes, until the carrots are soft.

Remove from the heat and add the coconut milk. Purée the soup in the pan using a stick blender, or transfer to a blender and blend until smooth.

Add a good squeeze of lime juice and then taste and adjust the seasoning, adding a dash of soy sauce or more lime juice to taste. Ladle into bowls and, if you like, add a swirl of coconut milk and sprinkle with chilli flakes and fresh coriander.

COOK'S TIP

Not all Thai red curry
paste is vegan, so check
the label when you shop.

Oxtail soup

A classic, hearty winter soup, this is very filling, and perfect for lunch on a crisp winter's day, served with warm bread.

Serves: 4 | **Prep:** 20 minutes | **Cook:** about 4 hours

1 tbsp vegetable oil

600–700g (1lb 5oz–1lb 9oz) oxtail, cut into pieces

300g (10½oz) onions, finely chopped

200g (7oz) carrots, finely chopped

2 sticks of celery, finely chopped

3 tbsp red wine

1 tbsp tomato purée

700ml (1¼ pints) beef stock

1 bay leaf

2 tbsp fresh thyme leaves

Salt and pepper

2 tbsp fresh chopped parsley (optional)

Preheat the oven to 190°C/180°C fan/gas 5.

Heat the oil in a large, heavy-based pan over a high heat and when it's very hot, add the oxtail pieces. Leave them – without stirring – until they start to colour and release from the bottom of the pan, then turn them over and brown well on all sides. Using a slotted spoon, transfer the oxtail to a roasting tin and place in the oven while you prepare the rest of the soup.

Add the onions, carrots and celery to the pan the oxtail was cooked in, reduce the heat to medium and fry, stirring frequently, for 10–15 minutes until softened and lightly coloured.

Add a good pinch of salt and pepper, then add the red wine and stir to deglaze the pan. Stir in the tomato purée and cook for a couple of minutes. Add the beef stock and the herbs and bring to the boil.

Return the oxtail to the pan. Reduce the heat to low, cover and simmer very gently for 3–3½ hours or until the meat is falling off the bones.

Remove the oxtail pieces and strip the meat off the bones, shredding any large pieces with a knife (see Cook's Tips).

Discard the bay leaf, then purée the soup in the pan using a stick blender, or transfer to a blender and blend until smooth. Add the meat from the oxtail and season well. Reheat the soup, ladle into bowls and sprinkle with parsley, if using.

COOK'S TIPS

Using a food processor makes quick work of finely chopping the vegetables.

Be careful when stripping the meat from the oxtail as it will be hot.

Cauliflower, turmeric and coconut soup

Turmeric gives this soup a glowing golden colour. It's quick and simple to make when you get back from a brisk walk – or, better still – prepare it before you set out and heat it through on your return.

Vegan | **Serves: 4** | **Prep: 20 minutes** | **Cook: 25 minutes**

1 tbsp vegetable oil

1 large onion, roughly chopped

1 tsp ground turmeric

2 tsp ground coriander

1 cauliflower, about 800–900g (1¾–2lb), roughly chopped

700ml (1¼ pints) hot vegetable stock or water

200ml (7fl oz) coconut milk

2 tbsp fresh chopped chives

Salt and pepper

Heat the oil in a large saucepan over a medium heat, add the onion and fry for 5–7 minutes, stirring from time to time, until soft and lightly coloured. Add the turmeric, coriander and cauliflower and fry for 2–3 minutes, stirring well. Add the hot stock or water and bring to the boil, then reduce the heat, cover and simmer for about 15 minutes until the cauliflower is tender.

Add the coconut milk, bring back to the boil, then remove from the heat. Purée the soup in the pan using a stick blender, or transfer to a blender and blend until smooth. Stir through most of the chopped chives and season to taste.

Ladle into bowls and top with the remaining chives.

COOK'S TIP

Slice the cauliflower stalks and use them in this soup. Remove the green outer leaves: you can shred them and use them in recipes requiring cabbage or kale, such as the Thai-style green curry soup (see page 16).

Roasted vegetable soup with apple slices

Roasted root vegetables and bulbs of garlic give this soup a rich sweetness.

Vegan | Serves: 4 | Prep: 20 minutes | Cook: 1 hour

400g (14oz) red onions, cut into chunks

200g (7oz) carrots, cut into chunks

200g (7oz) parsnips, peeled and cut into chunks

200g (7oz) sweet potatoes, peeled and cut into chunks

25ml (5 tsp) olive oil

3–4 sprigs of fresh thyme

2 garlic bulbs

850ml (1½ pints) hot vegetable stock or water

Salt and pepper

Apple slices

1 dessert apple, thinly sliced

1 tsp icing sugar

COOK'S TIP

The garlic must be completely roasted and soft to ensure it's sweet and fragrant – otherwise it will overpower the soup.

Preheat the oven to 160°C/150°C fan/gas 3 and line a baking sheet with non-stick baking paper.

First, place the slices of apple on the baking sheet and sprinkle over the icing sugar. Put in the oven for about 5 minutes, then turn the oven down to 130°C/120°C fan/gas ½, turn the apple slices over and bake until dry and starting to crisp (about 20–40 minutes). Leave to cool.

Turn the oven up to 200°C/190°C fan/gas 6 and line a large roasting tin with non-stick baking paper. Put the chopped vegetables into a bowl, add 1 tbsp of the oil and the thyme sprigs and toss to coat. Tip the vegetables into the lined roasting tin.

Put the garlic bulbs on a piece of foil, drizzle over the remaining 2 tsp oil, and then wrap the foil around the garlic to enclose it completely. Add to the roasting tin. Roast for 35–45 minutes until the vegetables are soft and lightly coloured. Gently squeeze the garlic bulbs to check that they are also soft (see Cook's Tip).

Unwrap the garlic and slice off the top of each bulb, then squeeze the soft flesh over the vegetables in the roasting tin.

Tip the vegetables and garlic into a large saucepan, discarding the thyme stalks. Season with salt and pepper, add the hot stock or water and bring to the boil. Remove the pan from the heat and purée the soup in the pan using a stick blender, or transfer to a blender and blend until smooth and creamy, adding extra salt and pepper to taste.

Ladle the soup into bowls and top with the apple slices.

Salads

Goat's cheese and tabbouleh salad

A Middle-Eastern-inspired salad with plenty of fresh herbs and moist, mildly spiced pearl barley. The addition of a crisp crouton topped with melting goat's cheese makes an original first course.

Vegetarian | Serves: 4 | Prep: 25 minutes | Cook: 45 minutes

200g (7oz) pearl barley, rinsed

3 tbsp cold-pressed rapeseed oil

½ tsp ground cinnamon

½ tsp ground mixed spice

Grated zest and juice of 1 lemon

1 tbsp honey

170g (6oz) tomatoes, finely diced

3 spring onions, thinly sliced

15g (½oz) fresh mint, finely chopped

40g (1½oz) fresh parsley, finely chopped

40g (1½oz) rocket

1 pomegranate, seeds only

Salt and pepper

Goat's cheese croutons

1 baguette, sliced

200g (7oz) vegetarian goat's cheese   -

Dressing

2 tsp honey

1 tsp cold-pressed rapeseed oil

1 tbsp white wine vinegar

1 tsp chopped fresh mint

Add the barley to a saucepan of boiling lightly salted water, bring back to the boil, then partly cover with a lid and simmer for 30–40 minutes, adding more boiling water, if needed, until the barley is cooked and tender.

Meanwhile, mix the oil, cinnamon, mixed spice, lemon zest and juice, and honey in a large bowl. Drain the barley in a colander, then add to the bowl, stir well and leave until cold.

Season the cold barley with plenty of salt and pepper, then add the tomatoes, spring onions, mint and parsley.

To make the croutons, place the bread slices on a baking sheet and toast until lightly golden.

To serve, add the rocket to the bowl with the salad and mix to distribute evenly. Divide between four serving plates.

Slice the goat's cheese, place some on each piece of toast and put back under the grill or into the oven until the cheese begins to melt. Place the goat's cheese croutons on top of your salad and scatter over the pomegranate seeds, or serve the croutons on the side.

Whisk all the dressing ingredients together in a bowl, drizzle over the salad and serve immediately.

Lentil and green bean salad with ginger dressing

This nutritious salad with its tangy ginger, sesame oil and lime dressing will boost energy levels and keep you feeling full all afternoon.

Vegan | Serves: 6 | Prep: 25 minutes | Cook: 25 minutes

250g (9oz) green lentils, rinsed

250g (9oz) broccoli

250g (9oz) green beans, trimmed and halved

150g (5½oz) carrots, peeled and cut into matchsticks

125g (4½oz) spring onions, thinly sliced

20g (¾oz) fresh coriander, roughly chopped

30g (1oz) sesame seeds

90g (3¼oz) young spinach leaves

Salt and pepper

Dressing

30g (1oz) root ginger, peeled and finely chopped

5 tbsp cold-pressed rapeseed oil

2 tbsp toasted sesame oil

1 tsp caster sugar

Grated zest and juice of 1 lime, plus more juice if needed

Add the lentils to a saucepan of boiling water, cover and simmer for about 20 minutes until just soft.

Cut the broccoli into bite-sized pieces; peel and chop the stalks. Place the broccoli and beans in a steamer set over the lentil pan, cover and cook for 3–4 minutes or until just tender. Plunge the vegetables into cold water to stop the cooking process, then drain and pat dry. (Alternatively, if you don't have a steamer, you can cook the broccoli and beans in a saucepan of boiling salted water for 1–2 minutes, then drain and refresh in cold water.)

Whisk all the dressing ingredients together in a bowl until creamy and emulsified.

Drain the lentils well and tip them into the dressing. Make sure the lentils are still hot when you add them to the dressing so they absorb more of the flavour. Mix well and season with salt and pepper.

Add the broccoli and beans to the lentils along with the carrots, spring onions and coriander; mix well. Season to taste, adding another squeeze of lime juice if needed.

Put the sesame seeds in a dry frying pan over a medium heat and toast for a few minutes, stirring frequently, until lightly golden.

Put the spinach in a serving bowl, add the lentil and vegetable mixture and sprinkle over the sesame seeds.

Potato, leek and almond salad with soured cream dressing

*Use new potatoes for this lovely summery salad. It's perfect for a party or
a picnic and it's delicious with poached or baked salmon or trout.*

Vegetarian | Serves: 4–6 | Prep: 15 minutes | Cook: 20 minutes

50g (1¾oz) flaked almonds

1 tbsp vegetable oil

400g (14oz) leeks, thinly sliced

500g (1lb 2oz) new potatoes, scrubbed and halved or quartered

Soured cream dressing

100g (3½oz) soured cream

100g (3½oz) mayonnaise

2 tbsp fresh chopped chives

1 tbsp fresh chopped tarragon

1 garlic clove, finely chopped

Grated zest and juice of 1 lemon

Salt and pepper

Put the almonds in a dry frying pan over a medium heat and toast for 3–5 minutes, stirring frequently, until starting to turn golden brown. Leave to cool.

Heat the oil in a frying pan over a high heat. Once hot, add the leeks and fry for 3–5 minutes until coloured and soft (see Cook's Tip). Leave to cool slightly.

Meanwhile, boil or steam the potatoes for 15–20 minutes until soft, then drain and refresh under cold running water.

To make the dressing, whisk all the ingredients together in a bowl. Taste and adjust the seasoning. Set aside.

Put the potatoes and leeks in a salad bowl, season with salt and pepper, then add the dressing and half the almonds and gently mix together. Scatter the remaining almonds over the top.

COOK'S TIP

Try to get a little charring on the leeks: this will add flavour and a bit of colour.

Harissa carrot salad

This brightly coloured salad, with flavours of Morocco, combines roast carrots, spiced roast chickpeas and oranges. It will look even more amazing if you use a variety of different coloured heritage carrots.

Vegan | Serves: 4 | Prep: 25 minutes | Cook: 45 minutes

500g (1lb 2oz) carrots, cut into bite-sized chunks

1 tbsp harissa

4 tsp vegetable oil

1 tbsp maple syrup

1 garlic clove, finely chopped

2 oranges

400g (14oz) can chickpeas, drained (keep the liquid, see Cook's Tip) and rinsed

80g (2¾oz) cashews

1 tsp ground cumin

2 tsp ground coriander

40g (1½oz) rocket

Salt and pepper

To serve

4 flour tortilla wraps or soft flatbreads

Preheat the oven to 180°C/170°C fan/gas 4 and line a roasting tin with non-stick baking paper.

Put the carrots in a bowl, add the harissa, half the oil, the maple syrup and garlic and mix well to coat. Tip the carrots into the roasting tin and roast for 20–30 minutes until just tender. Tip the carrots and any roasting juices into a bowl.

Cut the peel off the oranges, ensuring you also cut off all the pith, then cut the oranges into segments by sliding a small, sharp knife between the membranes. Add the orange segments to the bowl with the carrots and squeeze any juice from the leftover membranes into the bowl.

Put the chickpeas and cashews into the roasting tin, add the remaining vegetable oil, cumin, coriander, salt and pepper, stir well and roast for about 10 minutes until the nuts are just colouring. Add the chickpea and cashew mix to the bowl with the carrots.

If using tortilla wraps, turn the oven up to 220°C/200°C fan/gas 7. Cut the wraps into wedges, place on a baking sheet and bake for 5 minutes until crisp. Alternatively, warm the flatbreads according to the pack instructions.

Add the rocket to the carrot mixture and stir through. Season to taste. To serve, divide the salad between four plates and serve with the tortillas or flatbreads.

COOK'S TIP

Save the water from the can of chickpeas to glaze vegan pies or make a vegan mayonnaise (see page 50).

Pickled red cabbage salad
with smoked mackerel

A quick pickling technique gives a crunchy sweet-and-sour mix of red cabbage, fennel, carrot and apple. It contrasts perfectly with the smoked mackerel for a substantial lunchtime salad.

Serves: 4–6 | Prep: 25 minutes, plus 2 hours pickling time | Cook: 5 minutes

Pickling liquor

100ml (3½fl oz) white
   wine vinegar
100ml (3½fl oz) water
2 tbsp caster sugar
2 tsp coriander seeds,
   crushed
1 bay leaf
1 tsp salt
¼ tsp ground black pepper
4 tbsp fresh orange juice

Red cabbage salad

250g (9oz) red cabbage,
   shredded
150g (5½oz) carrots,
   peeled and grated
100g (3½oz) fennel, shredded
1 small dessert apple
2 tbsp fresh chopped parsley
1 tsp fresh thyme leaves

To serve

80g (2¾oz) salad leaves
1 smoked mackerel fillet
   per person
2 tbsp fresh chopped parsley

Place all the pickling liquor ingredients – except the orange juice – in a saucepan and bring to the boil, stirring until the sugar has dissolved. Remove from the heat, add the orange juice and leave to cool.

Put the shredded cabbage, carrots and fennel in a large bowl. Peel and roughly chop the apple and add to the bowl, then strain over the pickling liquor. Stir well and leave for at least 2 hours. You can make the pickled vegetables up to a day ahead; store in the fridge overnight.

To serve, add the parsley and thyme to the pickled vegetables and mix well. Divide the salad leaves among four serving plates. Place the pickled vegetables alongside the leaves. Flake the smoked mackerel into bite-sized pieces and add to the salad. Sprinkle with chopped parsley.

Roasted aubergine with chickpea salad and chilli caramelised nuts

Truly a feast for all the senses, with tender aromatic aubergines, a colourful chickpea salad, crunchy spicy nuts and a cooling tahini yogurt sauce.

Vegan | Serves: 4 | Prep: 30 minutes | Cook: 50 minutes

75ml (5 tbsp) dry white wine

4 tsp caster sugar

2.5cm (1 inch) piece of root
   ginger, peeled and chopped

½ garlic clove, chopped

2 tsp toasted sesame oil

2 tsp light soy sauce

2 tsp maple syrup

Pinch of dried chilli flakes

2 aubergines

1–2 tbsp vegetable oil

Roasted chickpea salad

400g (14oz) can chickpeas

1 tbsp ground coriander

½ red and ½ green pepper,
   deseeded

½ bunch of spring onions

Salt and pepper

Chilli caramelised nuts

60g (2¼oz) chopped nuts

40g (1½oz) caster sugar

Pinch of dried chilli flakes

Tahini sauce

30g (1oz) tahini

100g (3½oz) vegan yogurt

Grated zest and juice of 1 lime

Preheat the oven to 190°C/180°C fan/gas 5. Line a roasting tin with non-stick baking paper. For the roasted chickpea salad, drain and dry the chickpeas and put them in the lined tin. Sprinkle over the coriander and season with salt and pepper; stir to coat. Place in the oven for about 15 minutes until dried and lightly golden. Leave to cool in the roasting tin. Thinly slice the peppers and spring onions, put in a bowl with the cooled chickpeas, mix and set aside.

To make the sauce for the aubergines, put the white wine, sugar, ginger, garlic, sesame oil, soy sauce, syrup and chilli flakes in a saucepan over a medium heat. Bring to the boil and then immediately remove from the heat and set aside.

Cut the aubergines in half lengthways and score the flesh in a criss-cross pattern, cutting about halfway through the aubergines. Heat the vegetable oil in a large frying pan over a high heat and add the aubergines, cut-side down. Fry for about 3 minutes until golden, then turn and cook the other side. Transfer to a lined roasting tin, pour over the sauce and bake for about 30 minutes until soft. Baste the aubergines with the sauce from time to time.

To make the caramelised nuts, put the chopped nuts in a small heavy-based pan over a medium heat and cook until they begin to turn golden. Add the sugar and chilli and swirl the pan until the sugar has melted and caramelised. Turn out on to a plate and leave to cool.

To make the tahini sauce, put the tahini, yogurt and lime zest in a bowl and mix well, adding the lime juice to taste: the sauce should have the consistency of thick cream – add a little water if needed. Put to one side.

Place the roasted aubergines on serving plates. Add a portion of the chickpea salad, drizzle over the tahini sauce and scatter the caramelised nuts on top.

Coronation cauliflower and couscous salad

Inspired by the mild curry spices used for coronation chicken, this vegan dish uses cauliflower instead of chicken and a tasty couscous salad studded with red pepper, onion, sultanas and fresh herbs.

Vegan | Serves: 4 | Prep: 30 minutes | Cook: 25–30 minutes

Spicy roast cauliflower

1 tsp each of ground turmeric, ground ginger and ground cumin

3 tbsp water

1 cauliflower, 700–800g (1lb 9oz–1¾lb), chopped

Salt and pepper

Couscous salad

100g (3½oz) couscous

200ml (7fl oz) boiling water

Grated zest and juice of ½–1 lime

3 tbsp mango chutney

10g (⅓oz) each of fresh mint and fresh coriander, finely chopped

1 red pepper, deseeded and diced

½ red onion, finely diced

80g (2¾oz) sultanas

To serve

115g (4oz) salad leaves

4 tbsp vegan yogurt

50g (1¾oz) flaked almonds, lightly toasted

Preheat the oven to 200°C/190°C fan/gas 6 and line a roasting tin with non-stick baking paper.

For the spicy cauliflower, mix the spices with the water and a good pinch of salt and pepper in a large bowl. Add the chopped cauliflower and mix until well coated. Tip the cauliflower mixture into a roasting tin and roast for 25–30 minutes until tender and starting to crisp and colour. Remove from the oven and leave to cool.

Put the couscous in a bowl, add the boiling water, stir and then leave to stand for 10 minutes until the couscous is tender.

Add all the remaining couscous salad ingredients to the bowl, along with the roasted cauliflower, and stir through gently with a fork.

To serve, place the salad leaves in a serving bowl, add the cauliflower and couscous salad and top with a dollop of yogurt and the flaked almonds.

Brussels sprout, bacon and chestnut salad

If you think raw Brussels sprouts sound weird, this salad might change your mind. The earthy, nutty flavour of the sprouts goes so well with salty bacon, gentle chestnuts, tangy cranberries and an orange dressing.

Serves: 6 | Prep: 15 minutes | Cook: 10 minutes

200g (7oz) smoked bacon rashers or lardons

140g (5oz) cooked chestnuts, broken into small pieces (see Cook's Tip)

500g (1lb 2oz) raw Brussels sprouts, shredded

80g (2¾oz) dried cranberries

60g (2¼oz) young spinach leaves

Orange dressing

Grated zest and juice of 1 orange

4 tbsp cold-pressed rapeseed oil

Salt and pepper

Put the bacon in a large frying pan and heat gently until the fat begins to run, then increase the heat and cook until golden. Lift out of the pan using a slotted spoon, drain and chop. Set aside.

Add the chestnuts to the pan and stir over the heat for 2–3 minutes.

Put the sprouts and cranberries in a bowl, add the chestnuts and mix well.

To make the dressing, whisk the orange juice and zest with the oil and season with salt and pepper to taste. Pour over the sprout mixture.

Put the spinach in your serving bowl, top with the sprout mixture and finish with the chopped bacon.

COOK'S TIP

To use fresh chestnuts, cut a slit in the flat side of each one, then roast in a very hot oven (230°C/220°C fan/gas 8) for 8–10 minutes. Leave to cool, then peel off the shells and inner skins.

Roasted beetroot with walnuts and Stilton

Juicy roasted beetroot is marinated in a tangy dressing, contrasting with crisp raw beetroot, crunchy walnuts and creamy, savoury cheese to create a colourful and nutritious salad.

Vegetarian | Serves: 4 | Prep: 30 minutes, plus 2 hours marinating | Cook: about 1 hour

500g (1lb 2oz) red beetroot, scrubbed

1 sprig of rosemary

100g (3½oz) walnuts

4 tbsp orange juice

2 tbsp white wine vinegar

1 tbsp honey

100g (3½oz) golden beetroot

200g (7oz) candy-striped (Chioggia) beetroot

80g (2¾oz) Stilton

80g (2¾oz) full-fat cream cheese

2 tbsp Greek-style yogurt

1 tbsp finely chopped fresh dill

60g (2¼oz) rocket

Salt and pepper

Preheat the oven to 200°C/190°C fan/gas 6. Put the red beetroot on a sheet of foil with the rosemary, wrap the foil to make a sealed parcel and roast for 50–60 minutes until tender. Remove from the oven and leave to cool.

Toast the walnuts in the oven for 5 minutes. Set aside.

Peel the roasted beetroot and cut into bite-sized pieces. Mix together the orange juice, vinegar and honey and add to the roasted beetroot. Leave in the fridge to marinate for a couple of hours. Season to taste with salt and pepper.

Peel the golden beetroot and cut into matchsticks. Peel the Chioggia beetroot and cut into thin slices to show off the striped interior.

Mix the Stilton, cream cheese and yogurt in a bowl, add most of the dill (reserving a few fronds to garnish) and mix again. Season to taste.

Put the rocket on a serving plate. Arrange all three types of beetroot on top of the rocket. Using a teaspoon, dot small pieces of the cheese mixture across the top of the beetroot, followed by the toasted walnuts. Finish with a drizzle of the red beetroot dressing and some dill fronds.

COOK'S TIP

Golden and candy-striped beetroot make a really eye-catching salad but you can use an apple cut into matchsticks and thinly sliced red beetroot instead.

Light
Meals

Pea and mint scotch eggs

Scotch eggs have become a popular snack in recent years; some towns and cities even hold competitions among their local pubs and restaurants to find the best. With this recipe, vegetarians can enjoy them too.

Vegetarian | Serves: 4 | Prep: 30 minutes, plus chilling | Cook: 25 minutes

700g (1lb 9oz) frozen
  garden peas
4 tbsp finely chopped
  fresh mint
2 tbsp plain flour
4 eggs
Salt and pepper

To finish
2 tbsp plain flour
1 egg
100g (3½oz) fine dried
  breadcrumbs
vegetable oil, for
  deep frying

Put the frozen peas in a saucepan, add 2 tbsp water and bring to the boil, then cover the pan and reduce the heat. Cook for 10–15 minutes until the peas are slightly mushy, then use a potato masher to crush them a little (see Cook's Tip). Continue cooking until the peas are broken down and form clumps.

Tip the peas into a bowl. Add the mint and flour, season to taste with salt and pepper, stir well and leave to chill in the fridge for about 2 hours.

Meanwhile, put the eggs into a saucepan of cold water, bring to the boil and then reduce the heat and simmer for 5–6 minutes. Drain, crack the shells slightly and put the eggs into a bowl of ice-cold water for a few minutes before peeling away the shells. Set the eggs aside on a plate.

When the pea mixture is thoroughly chilled, divide it into four. Pat the eggs dry and then mould a quarter of the mixture around each egg, gently pressing to cover evenly. Place on a tray and chill in the fridge for 30–40 minutes.

To finish, put the flour on a saucer, crack the egg into a small bowl and beat until the white and yolk are combined. Put the breadcrumbs in a shallow dish. Roll the pea-coated eggs first in the flour, then in the beaten egg, and then in the breadcrumbs, coating them evenly.

Heat the oil to 170°C in a deep fat fryer or deep, heavy-based saucepan (a cube of bread should sizzle and brown, but not burn, as soon as it is dropped in). Once the oil is hot, carefully lower in the breaded eggs. Cook for 3–5 minutes, using a spoon to turn the eggs gently from time to time, until they're evenly browned.

Lift the eggs out of the oil and on to a tray lined with kitchen paper to drain any excess oil. Serve hot, or leave to cool and then store in the fridge for 1–2 days.

COOK'S TIP

Take care not to crush the peas too much or the mixture will become unworkable.

Cheese, bacon and chive scones

Breakfast, brunch, lunch or a hearty afternoon tea – these triangular savoury scones are welcome at any time of day ... or night.

Gluten-free | Makes 12 scones | Prep: 20 minutes | Cook: 25 minutes

100g (3½oz) bacon

Vegetable oil, for greasing

500g (1lb 2oz) gluten-free self-raising flour, plus extra for dusting

125g (4½oz) butter, diced

15–20g (½–¾oz) fresh chives, snipped

200g (7oz) Cheddar cheese, grated

1 egg, beaten

400ml (14fl oz) milk

Salt and pepper

Put the bacon in a large frying pan and heat gently until the fat begins to run, then increase the heat and cook until golden. Chop and leave to cool.

Preheat the oven to 200°C/190°C fan/gas 6. Lightly oil a baking sheet.

Put the flour, butter and some salt and pepper in a bowl and rub in using your fingertips or an electric mixer until the mixture resembles fine crumbs. Add the bacon, chives and most of the cheese (reserving a little to top the scones) and stir through.

Mix the egg with three-quarters of the milk. Gradually add the liquid to the dry ingredients, and then slowly add the remaining milk, mixing until you have a loose, sticky dough.

Tip the dough on to a lightly floured surface (see Cook's Tips). Divide the dough into three equal portions, shape into balls and flatten slightly. Carefully transfer to the baking sheet. Score each dough round into four wedges (don't cut all the way through) and sprinkle the reserved cheese on top, pressing lightly.

Bake for about 20 minutes until risen, golden and firm to the touch. Leave to cool slightly before serving.

COOK'S TIPS

For a vegetarian cheese and chive scone, simply leave out the bacon.

To get a good texture, the dough needs to be very wet: use just enough flour on your work surface to prevent the dough from sticking.

Beetroot, carrot and spring onion fritters

These crisp vegetable fritters are very versatile: serve them as a first course or snack, or with a selection of salads as a main meal.

Vegan | **Serves: 4** | **Prep: 20 minutes** | **Cook: 15–20 minutes**

200g (7oz) gram flour

200g (7oz) raw beetroot, peeled and grated

200g (7oz) carrot, peeled and grated

1 bunch of spring onions, finely chopped

2 tbsp vegetable oil

Salt and pepper

Vegan mayonnaise

75ml (5 tbsp) aquafaba (chickpea water)

1½ tsp English mustard

Grated zest and juice of ½ lemon

250ml (9fl oz) vegetable oil

1–2 tbsp fincly chopped fresh tarragon

Preheat the oven to 190°C/180°C fan/gas 5.

Put the gram flour in a bowl, add a pinch of salt and pepper and stir to mix. Add the beetroot, carrot and spring onions and mix again. Add just enough water to bind the mixture together (you may not need any). Set aside.

To make the vegan mayonnaise, put all the ingredients except the tarragon in a jug, add a good pinch of salt and blitz using a stick blender until thick and creamy. Stir in the tarragon and set aside in the fridge.

Heat the oil in a large frying pan over a medium heat. Once the oil is hot, divide the fritter mixture into four and add to the pan (see Cook's Tip). Fry for 2–3 minutes until the bottoms set and start to go crisp. Carefully flip the fritters and cook for 2–3 minutes on the other side.

Transfer the fritters to a baking sheet and place in the oven for about 10 minutes to ensure they are cooked through. Serve hot, with vegan mayo and salad on the side.

COOK'S TIP

Make sure the oil is hot before adding the fritter mixture; to test, drop half a teaspoonful of the mixture into the oil – it should immediately sizzle.

Pea, broccoli and rocket tart

Rich cheese pastry holds a fresh-tasting filling in vibrant shades of green – a perfect tart for a spring or summer lunch.

Vegetarian | Serves: 6–8 | Prep: 30 minutes, plus chilling | Cook: about 1 hour

Cheese shortcrust pastry

225g (8oz) plain flour, plus extra for dusting

A pinch of salt

115g (4oz) butter, diced, plus extra for greasing

50g (1¾oz) vegetarian Cheddar cheese, grated

1 egg, beaten

1–2 tbsp milk

Filling

150g (5½oz) broccoli

100g (3½oz) peas

50g (1¾oz) rocket, roughly chopped

2 tbsp finely chopped fresh mint

150g (5½oz) vegetarian Cheddar cheese, grated (optional)

150ml (5fl oz) milk

100ml (3½fl oz) double cream

5 eggs

Salt and pepper

To make the pastry, put the flour, salt and butter in a bowl and rub in using your fingertips or an electric mixer until the mixture resembles fine crumbs. Stir in the cheese, then mix in the egg and just enough milk to make a smooth, soft dough.

Lightly knead the dough, then roll out on a lightly floured surface until a little larger than a deep, 23cm (9 inch) buttered tart tin. Lift the pastry over the rolling pin and press into the tin. Prick the base all over with a fork, then chill for 20–30 minutes.

Preheat the oven to 190°C/180°C fan/gas 5. Line the pastry with a circle of non-stick baking paper, fill with baking beans and bake for 10 minutes. Remove the paper and beans and cook for about 5 more minutes until the pastry is crisp and dry. Set aside.

Meanwhile, make the filling. Cut the broccoli into bite-sized pieces, peel and chop the stalks, then blanch in boiling water until just tender. Drain, refresh in cold water, then drain well and pat dry. Boil the peas for 2 minutes; drain well. Put the vegetables in a bowl and gently mix in the rocket and mint.

Turn the oven down to 180°C/170°C fan/gas 4.

Spoon the vegetables into the pastry case and sprinkle over half the cheese, if using. Whisk the milk, cream and eggs together in a jug and season with salt and pepper. Gently pour over the vegetables in the pastry case, then sprinkle over the remaining cheese. Bake for 30–40 minutes until the top is golden brown and the filling is set, but with a slight wobble. Leave to stand for at least 10 minutes before slicing.

Courgette, fennel, olive and feta frittata

This Italian-style omelette is cooked more slowly than its French counterpart. It can be enjoyed warm from the pan, or cut into wedges to eat al fresco.

Vegetarian | **Serves: 4** | **Prep: 15 minutes** | **Cook: 30 minutes**

250g (9oz) potatoes, scrubbed and cut into 1cm (½ inch) cubes

2 tbsp olive oil

200g (7oz) courgettes, diced

150g (5½oz) fennel, thinly sliced

6 eggs, whisked

30g (1oz) pitted black olives, halved

125g (4½oz) vegetarian feta cheese, diced

2 tbsp fresh chopped parsley

Salt and pepper

Add the potatoes to a saucepan of boiling water and cook for 5 minutes until just tender; do not overcook. Drain and set aside.

Heat the oil in a large frying pan – about 23cm (9 inch) – over a medium–high heat. When hot, add the potatoes, courgettes and fennel and fry for 5–10 minutes until they begin to soften and colour.

Preheat the grill to high.

Mix the eggs with the olives, feta and parsley, season with salt and pepper, and pour over the vegetables in the pan. Reduce the heat to low, cover and cook for about 10 minutes until the bottom is set and golden (see Cook's Tips).

Put the pan under the grill and cook for about 3–4 minutes until the eggs are cooked through.

Loosen the edges of the frittata with a spatula, then cover the pan with a large plate and, holding the handle with an oven glove, turn it upside down. Shake to release the frittata and then remove the pan. Cut into wedges and serve warm or cold with a salad on the side.

COOK'S TIPS

Cover the pan with a lid or some foil while cooking: this helps to prevent sticking and keeps the frittata moist.

If serving cold, this can be made a day in advance and kept in the fridge.

Basil and goat's cheese twists

These rustic bread twists are not difficult to make: they're great for brunch, or served alongside soup for lunch. Try different fillings such as fresh thyme and sun-dried tomatoes.

Vegetarian | Makes 12 | Prep: 30 minutes, plus rising | Cook: 20–25 minutes

500g (1lb 2oz) strong white flour, plus extra for dusting
1 tbsp caster sugar
2 tsp (7g sachet) fast-action dried yeast
½ tsp salt
About 300ml (½ pint) warm water
70g (2½oz) butter, diced

Filling
170g (6oz) butter, softened
50g (1¾oz) fresh basil, roughly chopped
250g (9oz) vegetarian goat's cheese, chopped into small chunks

Put the flour, sugar, yeast and salt in the bowl of a mixer and beat with the dough hook on low speed. Gradually add the warm water and mix until you have a smooth, soft dough. If you don't have an electric mixer, stir with a wooden spoon, then bring the dough together with your hands.

Add the butter and continue to knead the dough for about 4 minutes in the mixer, or turn the dough on to a lightly floured work surface and knead for 8–10 minutes until it feels springy. The dough will be sticky at first, but don't be tempted to add more flour (though you may need to lightly flour your hands) as the dough will gradually become smooth and soft again.

Tip the dough out on to a lightly floured surface and knead into a ball. Place in a floured bowl, cover and leave in a warm place for about 1 hour until doubled in size – or leave overnight in the fridge.

Line a large baking sheet with non-stick baking paper. Place the dough on a floured surface and roll out to a rectangle about 48 x 30cm (19 x 12 inches), with the long edge facing you.

For the filling, mix the butter and basil together and spread over the dough, then scatter over the goat's cheese. Fold in half from top to bottom and press down gently.

Cut the dough into 24 strips, each 2cm (¾ inches) wide. Take two strips, twist them together and place on the lined baking sheet. Repeat with the remaining strips. Cover and leave in a warm place for about 40 minutes until the twists are risen and puffy. Preheat the oven to 200°C/190°C fan/gas 6.

Bake the twists for 20–25 minutes until golden and risen. To check that they are cooked, lift one up and tap the bottom: it should sound hollow when done.

COOK'S TIP

For a vegan version, replace the butter with dairy-free margarine and the goat's cheese with vegan cheese.

Summer veg filo tarts

Serve these crisp tarts with coleslaw or potato salad for a light meal, try them as a first course for a summer supper party, or put a plate of them on the table at an al fresco buffet or a picnic.

Vegan | Makes 10–12 | Prep: 15 minutes, plus chilling | Cook: 35 minutes

1 tbsp olive oil, plus extra to brush the filo

250g (9oz) red onions, thinly sliced

250g (9oz) carrots, peeled and cut into small dice

1 red pepper, deseeded and cut into small dice

500g (1lb 2oz) tomatoes, diced

100g (3½oz) tomato purée

300g (10½oz) courgettes, grated

300g (10½oz) peas

15–20g (½–¾oz) fresh chives, snipped

1 pack, about 250g (9oz), of filo pastry (you will need 10–12 sheets)

Salt and pepper

Topping (optional)

20g (¾oz) dairy-free margarine

1 bunch, about 125g (4½oz), of spring onions, finely chopped

Heat the oil in a large saucepan over a medium heat, add the onions, carrots and red pepper and fry for 10–15 minutes until softened and lightly coloured.

Add the tomatoes and tomato purée, stir well, then increase the heat and cook for about 5 minutes, stirring continuously to prevent sticking, until the mixture thickens slightly.

Add the courgettes, peas and chives, season with salt and pepper and stir well. Remove from the heat and leave to cool.

Preheat the oven to 200°C/190°C fan/gas 6 and put a baking sheet in the oven to heat. Lightly oil a 12-hole deep muffin tin.

Lay out a sheet of filo pastry and brush half of it with a little oil, fold over and then cut in half across the middle. Brush one half with more oil and place the other half on top, at an angle. Place the filo in one muffin hole, pressing it down into the bottom of the tin and leaving the top of the pastry standing proud out of the tin. Repeat with the remaining filo sheets.

Divide the vegetable mixture between the filo cases, then put the muffin tin on the hot baking sheet and bake for 12–15 minutes until the pastry is golden brown and crisp.

Meanwhile, to make the topping, melt the dairy-free margarine in a pan over a low–medium heat, add the spring onions and fry until they begin to soften. Remove the tarts from the oven and spoon a little of the topping on to each one.

Pork, apple and sage pies

Mini pork pies are a favourite lunchbox treat, perfect for a picnic or a family gathering at any time of year.

Makes 6 | Prep: 40 minutes | Cook: 50 minutes

Filling

340g (12oz) diced pork, finely chopped

100g (3½oz) sausage meat

1 tbsp dried sage

½ tart apple, such as Granny Smith, peeled, cored and chopped

Salt and pepper

Hot-water crust pastry

125g (4½oz) lard, plus extra for greasing

170ml (6fl oz) water

300g (10½oz) strong white flour

½ tsp salt

1 egg, beaten, to glaze

COOK'S TIPS

You will need to work quickly while the dough is warm; once it has cooled it will be unworkable. Cover the dough with a warm, damp tea towel to prevent it from cooling too quickly.

To make the filling, put all the ingredients into a bowl and mix thoroughly. Set aside.

Preheat the oven to 200°C/190°C fan/gas 6 and put a baking sheet in the oven to heat. Thoroughly grease a 6-hole deep muffin tin and line with discs of non-stick baking paper.

To make the pastry, melt the lard with the water in a saucepan over a medium heat. When the lard has melted, tip in the flour and salt, remove from the heat and mix until you have a soft dough (see Cook's Tips).

Take a piece of the dough, approximately 55g (2oz), roll into a ball, then flatten in the palm of your hand and place in a hole of the muffin tin. Shape it into the tin, trying to keep the pastry an even thickness, with a little lip above the top of each hole. Repeat until you have filled all the muffin holes.

Pack with the filling, pushing down to keep it as compact as possible and mounding the top slightly.

Take a ball of pastry, approximately 30g (1oz), flatten into a disc, and place on top of the filling, pressing the edges down on the pastry lip and smoothing the edges. Use a knife to make a small hole in the top of each pie. Glaze with the beaten egg.

Put the muffin tin on the hot baking sheet and bake for 45–50 minutes until the pastry is golden and crisp and the filling is cooked. Test the filling with a skewer: it should be piping hot. Leave to cool slightly before removing the pies from the tins.

Smoked salmon and watercress quiche

Slightly salty smoked salmon, the distinctive grassy, anise flavour of dill and peppery watercress are a dream team; here they meet in a creamy quiche with a buttery pastry crust, to enjoy hot or cold.

Serves: 6–8 | Prep: 20 minutes, plus chilling | Cook: about 1 hour

Pastry

225g (8oz) plain flour,
   plus extra for dusting
115g (4oz) butter, diced,
   plus extra for greasing
A pinch of salt
2–3 tbsp cold water

Filling

200g (7oz) smoked salmon
70g (2½oz) watercress
½ bunch of spring onions,
   thinly sliced
2 tbsp finely chopped
   fresh dill
150ml (5fl oz) milk
100ml (3½fl oz) double
   cream
5 eggs
Salt and pepper

To make the pastry, put the flour and butter into a bowl and rub together until the mixture resembles fine crumbs. Add the salt and just enough cold water to bring the mixture together into a dough. Wrap in a clean, dry tea towel or beeswax wrap and chill for 20–30 minutes.

Preheat the oven to 190°C/180°C fan/gas 5. Lightly butter a deep, 23cm (9 inch) tart tin.

On a lightly floured surface, roll out the pastry to around 3mm (⅛ inch) thick and use to line the buttered tart tin. Prick the base all over with a fork, and then line the pastry with a circle of non-stick baking paper; fill with baking beans and bake for 10 minutes. Remove the paper and beans and cook for about 5 more minutes or until the pastry is crisp and dry. Set aside.

Turn the oven down to 180°C/170°C fan/gas 4.

To make the filling, tear the salmon into bite-sized pieces. Discard any very large or woody stalks from the watercress and roughly chop the rest. Put the salmon and watercress in a bowl, add the spring onions and dill and gently mix, then spoon into the pastry case.

Whisk the milk, cream and eggs together in a jug, season with salt and pepper and then gently pour into the pastry case. Bake for 30–40 minutes until the top is golden and the filling is set, but with a slight wobble. Leave to stand for at least 10 minutes before slicing.

Spiced cauliflower and potato parcels

These crisp, veggie-packed parcels are like samosas but are much healthier because they're baked rather than deep-fried. Serve as a hearty first course, a satisfying lunch or supper, or simply enjoy as a snack.

Vegan | **Makes 20** | **Prep: 30 minutes** | **Cook: 25–30 minutes**

200g (7oz) cauliflower,
 cut into small florets
200g (7oz) potato, peeled
 and diced
1 tbsp vegetable oil, plus
 extra to brush the filo
1 onion, finely sliced
100g (3½oz) sweet potato,
 peeled and grated
85g (3oz) vegan tikka paste
2 tbsp dry white wine
215g (7½oz) can chickpeas,
 drained and rinsed
70g (2½oz) sultanas
Juice of 1 lime
1 pack of filo pastry
 about 250g (9oz)
Salt and pepper

Mint yogurt
600g (1lb 5oz) coconut
 milk (non-dairy) yogurt
30g (1oz) fresh mint,
 finely chopped

Lightly steam the cauliflower and potato for 5–7 minutes or until just tender. Remove and drain.

Place a saucepan over a medium heat, add the oil, then add the onion and sweet potato and fry for 8–10 minutes until softened. Add the tikka paste, stir well and cook for 1–2 more minutes.

Add the wine to the pan and stir, then add the cauliflower, potato, chickpeas and sultanas and cook for a few minutes until everything is tender and most of the liquid has been absorbed. Add the lime juice and stir through. Taste and adjust the seasoning, and then set aside.

Preheat the oven to 230°C/220°C fan/gas 8.

Lay out a sheet of filo and cut in half along the length. Brush with oil and place a spoonful of the cauliflower mixture at one end. Fold the end of the pastry over to form a triangle with the cauliflower mixture inside. Fold the pastry over again, maintaining the triangle shape, and continue folding until you have folded all the pastry over and you have a triangular parcel. Brush with a little oil and put to one side while you repeat with the remaining filo.

Place the parcels on a baking sheet and bake for 2 minutes, then turn them over and turn the oven down to 200°C/190°C fan/gas 6 and bake for a further 5 minutes.

Mix the yogurt with the mint and season to taste with salt and pepper.

Serve hot, with the yogurt sauce and some salad.

Squash, feta and sage filo bake

Crisp and light filo pastry with a filling of silky butternut squash and creamy feta makes a laid-back bake for lunch or supper.

Vegetarian | Serves: 6 | Prep: 30 minutes | Cook 30–40 minutes

85g (3oz) butter, melted

300g (10½oz) butternut squash, peeled

1 tbsp finely chopped fresh sage

1 tsp ground cumin

200g (7oz) vegetarian feta cheese

1 egg

1 pack of filo pastry, about 250g (9oz)

Salt and pepper

Preheat the oven to 200°C/190°C fan/gas 6 and brush a small roasting tin – about 28 x 18cm (11 x 7 inches) – with melted butter.

Cut the squash in half, remove the seeds, then thinly slice. Put the squash slices in a bowl with the sage and cumin, season with salt and pepper and mix well.

Put 150g (5½oz) of the feta cheese into a food processor with the egg and blitz to form a smooth paste.

Unroll the filo pastry. Lay a sheet of filo on the roasting tin and brush with melted butter. Repeat with the remaining sheets of filo, overlapping the sheets if necessary to cover the baking sheet evenly. Bunch up the pastry along the edges to create a crust.

Spread the feta and egg mixture over the pastry. Lay the slices of seasoned butternut squash evenly over the feta mixture, tipping in any seasoning left in the bowl. Crumble the remaining feta cheese over the squash.

Bake for 30–40 minutes until the pastry is crisp and golden brown. Leave in the tin to cool slightly, then cut into pieces and serve warm or cold.

Roasted beetroot, kale and Brie quiche

Gluten-free quiche? The secret's in the sweet-potato crust that replaces the traditional pastry. Filled with beetroot and kale, you've got half your daily rainbow of veg on one plate.

Gluten-free, Vegetarian | Serves: 6–8 | Prep: 30 minutes | Cook: 45–50 minutes, plus 1 hour for roasting

400g (14oz) beetroot in their skins, scrubbed

2 tsp cold-pressed rapeseed oil

200g (7oz) red onions, roughly chopped

100g (3½oz) kale, thinly sliced

1 sprig of rosemary, leaves finely chopped

250g (9oz) vegetarian Brie, cubed

100ml (3½fl oz) milk

85ml (3fl oz) double cream

4 eggs

Sweet potato crust

400g (14oz) sweet potato, peeled and grated

1 egg, beaten

50g (1¾oz) vegetarian Cheddar cheese, grated

A pinch of dried chilli flakes

Salt and pepper

Preheat the oven to 200°C/190°C fan/gas 6. Put the beetroot on a sheet of foil, add a splash of water and then wrap the foil to make a sealed parcel. Bake for 50–60 minutes until tender. Remove from the oven and leave to cool.

To make the crust, put the sweet potato in a sieve and squeeze out as much liquid as you can. Place the sweet potato in a bowl and mix in the egg, cheese, chilli flakes and a little salt and pepper.

Line the base and sides of a loose-bottomed, deep, 23cm (9 inch) tart tin with non-stick baking paper (this helps to prevent any leaks). Spoon the sweet-potato mixture into the tin and use the back of a spoon to press into an even layer over the base and up the sides, making sure it's well compressed. Keep back a little of the mixture to patch any holes after baking.

Bake for 15–20 minutes until the potato is set and beginning to crisp around the edges. Check for any holes or cracks and patch with the reserved potato mixture. Turn the oven down to 180°C/170°C fan/gas 4.

Place a frying pan over a medium–high heat, add the oil, then fry the onions for about 10 minutes until beginning to brown. Meanwhile, put the kale into a saucepan of boiling water for 5 minutes, then drain in a colander, refresh in cold water, drain well and pat dry. Rub the skins off the beetroot and cut into small bite-sized pieces. Pat dry with kitchen paper. Put the beetroot, onions, kale, rosemary and half the Brie in a bowl and gently stir until evenly mixed. Spoon into the sweet potato crust.

Whisk the milk, cream and eggs together in a jug and season with salt and pepper. Pour over the vegetable mixture. Scatter over the remaining Brie. Bake for 35–40 minutes or until golden and just set. Leave to cool slightly before removing from the tin and cutting into wedges.

Croque monsieur

This French bistro favourite is the ultimate cheese and ham toastie, topped with a creamy sauce.
Serve as an anytime snack or as a lunch or supper dish with a green or tomato salad.

Serves: 2 | Prep: 20 minutes | Cook: 15 minutes

White sauce
20g (¾oz) butter
20g (¾oz) plain flour
200ml (7fl oz) hot milk
A pinch of grated nutmeg
Salt and pepper

To assemble
4 slices of bread
20g (¾oz) butter, melted
2–3 tsp Dijon mustard
2 slices of ham
85g (3oz) mature Cheddar
  cheese, grated

To make the sauce, melt the butter in a small pan and stir in the flour until the mixture forms a paste. Gradually whisk in the hot milk, then cook for 4–6 minutes, whisking continuously until the sauce has thickened. Season to taste with nutmeg, salt and pepper and set aside.

Preheat the grill and preheat the oven to 200°C/190°C fan/gas 6. Line a baking sheet with non-stick baking paper.

Brush the bread on one side with melted butter and place under the grill to toast the buttered side. Remove from the grill, turn the slices over and spread the mustard on the untoasted side of two slices, followed by a little of the sauce, a slice of ham and about half of the cheese. Top with the other slice of bread, placing the untoasted side on the cheese.

Place the sandwiches on the lined baking sheet. Top with the remaining sauce and sprinkle over the rest of the cheese. Bake for about 10 minutes until golden and bubbling. Cut in half and serve immediately.

COOK'S TIPS

Let the sauce cool and thicken slightly before assembling.

For a vegetarian version, replace the ham with chopped sun-dried (or oven-dried) tomatoes and a little oregano.

Add a fried egg on top *et voilà*, you've got a croque madame.

Pear, walnut and Stilton quiches

These little quiches are made in a muffin tin. They're brilliant on a party buffet table, or serve them for lunch with a mixed-leaf salad and crisp coleslaw.

Vegetarian | Makes 12 | Prep: 30 minutes, plus chilling | Cook: 20 minutes

Pastry
Vegetable oil, for greasing
250g (9oz) plain flour,
    plus extra for dusting
125g (4½oz) butter, diced
A pinch of salt
2–3 tbsp cold water

Filling
150ml (5fl oz) milk
3 eggs
150g (5½oz) pears,
    peeled, cored and
    roughly chopped
70g (2½oz) walnuts,
    roughly chopped
150g (5½oz) vegetarian
    Stilton, crumbled
Salt and pepper

Lightly oil a 12-hole non-stick muffin tin and line each with a small disc of non-stick baking paper.

To make the pastry, put the flour and butter into a bowl and rub together until it resembles fine crumbs. Add the salt and just enough cold water to bring the mixture together into a dough.

On a lightly floured surface, roll out the dough to 3mm (⅛ inch) thick and use a 10cm (4 inch) cutter to cut out 12 discs. Press the discs into the muffin tin, using a pastry offcut dipped in flour to press the pastry into the corners. Put the tin in the fridge to chill for 20–30 minutes.

Preheat the oven to 190°C/180°C fan/gas 5 and put a baking sheet into the oven to heat.

To make the filling, whisk together the milk and eggs in a measuring jug and season with salt and pepper. Divide the pears, walnuts and Stilton between the pastry cases, then pour in the egg mixture. Carefully transfer the muffin tin to the hot baking sheet and bake for 20 minutes until the filling is set and the pastry is crisp. Serve hot or at room temperature.

COOK'S TIP
Instead of Stilton, try these with vegetarian goat's cheese.

Mushroom and cranberry rolls

Sausage rolls are a Christmas-party staple for many, and there's no reason for vegetarians to feel left out with these rich mushroom, sage and onion filled pastries. And remember, a veggie roll is not just for Christmas!

Vegan | Makes 6 | Prep: 20 minutes | Cook: 25–30 minutes

150g (5½oz) onions,
    roughly chopped
2 garlic cloves, peeled
300g (10½oz) mushrooms
215g (7½oz) can chickpeas
    – 130g (4½oz) drained
    weight
150g (5½oz) polenta
1 tbsp dried sage
70g (2½oz) dried
    cranberries
500g (1lb 2oz) vegan
    puff pastry
Plain flour, for dusting
Salt and pepper

Preheat the oven to 200°C/190°C fan/gas 6. Line a baking sheet with non-stick baking paper.

Put the onions, garlic and mushrooms in a food processor and blitz until finely chopped. Transfer to a large bowl.

Drain the chickpeas – reserving the liquid to glaze the rolls – and rinse. Put the chickpeas in the processor and pulse until roughly chopped but some texture remains. Add to the bowl with the mushrooms, then add the polenta and sage, season well with salt and pepper and mix thoroughly. Add the cranberries and stir through.

Roll out the pastry on a lightly floured surface and trim to a rectangle 45 x 15cm (18 x 6 inches). Wet the long edges with a little water.

Spoon the mushroom mixture in a thick strip along the pastry, slightly to one side, moulding it to a sausage shape with your hands. Fold the pastry over the filling and press the edges together to seal. If you like, you can roll the pastry over so that the join is underneath. Cut into six rolls. Place on the lined baking sheet and score the tops diagonally with a knife, then brush with the reserved chickpea liquid.

Bake for 25–30 minutes until golden and risen. Transfer to a wire rack to cool.

COOK'S TIP

The mushroom mixture might seem a little wet, but the polenta will absorb the moisture as it cooks.

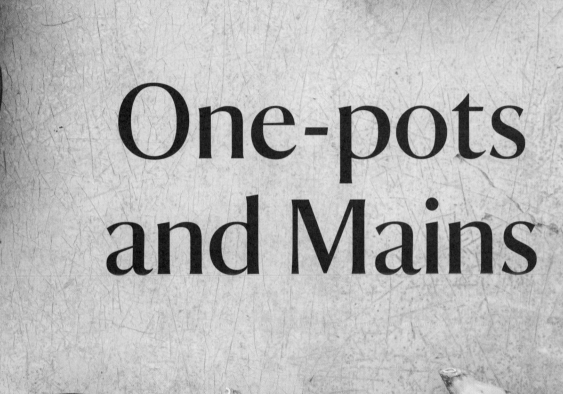

One-pots and Mains

Spring vegetable pasta alfredo

We've given the classic Italian dish of fettuccine all'Alfredo a tasty twist by adding a variety of vegetables and herbs. The sauce is traditionally served with tagliatelle, but any type of pasta will be just as good.

Vegetarian | Serves: 4 | Prep: 30 minutes | Cook: 20 minutes

150g (5½oz) asparagus, roughly chopped

100g (3½oz) broccoli, cut into small pieces

100g (3½oz) broad beans

100g (3½oz) mangetout, sliced

½ bunch of spring onions, sliced

1 small red onion, thinly sliced (optional)

Alfredo sauce

30g (1oz) butter

1 garlic clove, finely chopped

85ml (3fl oz) double cream

120ml (4fl oz) milk

100g (3½oz) vegetarian Cheddar cheese, grated

10g (⅓oz) fresh parsley, finely chopped

10g (⅓oz) fresh oregano, finely chopped

Salt and pepper

To serve

200g (7oz) tagliatelle

100g (3½oz) vegetarian Cheddar cheese, grated

2 tbsp fresh chopped basil

Place the asparagus, broccoli, broad beans, mangetout and spring onions in a steamer and steam for 5 minutes, until just starting to cook but still firm. Remove and refresh in chilled water, drain and leave to dry. Mix through the red onion, if using.

To make the sauce, place a large saucepan over a low heat, add the butter and garlic and fry for about 3 minutes until the garlic is beginning to soften and colour lightly.

Stir in the cream and milk and bring to the boil, then reduce the heat and add the grated Cheddar, parsley and oregano. Simmer for 5–10 minutes, stirring frequently, until the cheese has melted and the sauce is slightly thickened. Season to taste.

Add the tagliatelle to a large saucepan of boiling water. Cook for 10–12 minutes, until just tender, and then drain.

Add the cooked tagliatelle and vegetables to the alfredo sauce and heat through over a low heat for 2–3 minutes. Spoon into four serving bowls, top with grated cheese and fresh basil and serve immediately.

Lamb hotpot

We've packed extra veggies into this version of the traditional dish of tender lamb topped with crisp potatoes. It's a meal in itself, or you can add a generous side dish of green vegetables.

Serves: 4 | Prep: 30 minutes | Cook: over 3 hours

600g (1lb 5oz) leg
   of lamb, diced
1 tbsp cornflour
1 tbsp vegetable oil
1 large onion, roughly
   chopped
1 stick of celery, roughly
   chopped
150g (5½oz) carrots, peeled
   and roughly chopped
100g (3½oz) swede,
   roughly chopped
2 tbsp red wine
2 tsp English mustard
A pinch of grated nutmeg
1 tbsp fresh chopped
   rosemary
1 tbsp fresh thyme leaves
200ml (7fl oz) lamb or
   beef stock
500g (1lb 2oz) potatoes,
   peeled and thinly sliced
Salt and pepper

Preheat the oven to 160°C/150°C fan/gas 3.

Toss the lamb in the cornflour. Heat the oil in a large casserole dish over a medium–high heat, add the lamb and fry – in batches, if needed, to avoid overcrowding the pan – until browned all over. Transfer to a plate using a slotted spoon.

Add the onion, celery, carrots, swede, red wine, mustard, nutmeg, rosemary and thyme to the casserole and fry, stirring, for about 5 minutes.

Return the lamb and any juices to the casserole, pour in the stock, stir well and bring to the boil. Take the pan off the heat and arrange the potato slices in layers on top of the meat and vegetables, seasoning the layers with salt and pepper. Cover the casserole with a lid or foil, place in the oven, and cook for 1½–2 hours. Test the potatoes and meat to ensure they're tender.

Turn up the oven to 200°C/190°C fan/gas 6. Put the casserole back in the oven, uncovered, for 20–30 minutes until the potatoes are browned and beginning to crisp up.

Serve hot with a side dish of green vegetables.

COOK'S TIP

You can cook the lamb in the lower part of your oven while cooking other dishes on a higher shelf.

Pork stroganoff

A comforting bowl of smoky spiced pork in a creamy sauce.
Serve with rice, pasta or mashed potato.

Serves: 4 | Prep: 25 minutes, plus marinating | Cook: about 2 hours

600g (1lb 5oz) diced pork

1 tsp smoked paprika

¼ tsp cayenne pepper

½ tsp coarsely ground
  black pepper

1 tbsp vegetable oil

400g (14oz) onions,
  roughly chopped

2 garlic cloves, roughly
  chopped

4 tbsp red wine

250g (9oz) mushrooms,
  roughly chopped

1 tbsp wholegrain mustard

1 tsp brandy

85ml (3fl oz) double cream

25–30g (1oz) fresh parsley,
  roughly chopped

Juice of ½–1 lemon

1 tbsp cornflour

Salt and pepper

Put the pork, smoked paprika, cayenne pepper and coarsely ground black pepper in a large bowl and mix well, using your hands to work the seasonings into the meat. Leave to stand for at least 30 minutes.

Heat the oil in a large, flameproof casserole dish over a medium heat. Add the onions, garlic and a good pinch of salt, then fry for 15–20 minutes, stirring occasionally, until the onions are soft.

Turn the heat up to high, tip the pork into the pan and fry, stirring, until the pork is browned all over.

Add the wine and just enough water to cover, bring to the boil and then reduce the heat to very low. Cover and simmer for 1–1½ hours until the meat is tender (see Cook's Tip).

Add the mushrooms, stir well and simmer for a further 10 minutes

Remove from the heat and add the mustard, brandy, cream, parsley and a good squeeze of lemon juice. Stir well and return to the heat. Mix the cornflour with a little water until smooth. Stir into the creamy sauce, bring back to the boil and simmer for a couple of minutes until thickened. Taste and adjust the seasoning, spoon into bowls and serve.

COOK'S TIP

Keep the pork at a very
gentle simmer: if the heat
is too high, the meat
will toughen.

Sweet potato and cauliflower curry pies

Serve these tasty little pies with seasonal veg or peas, and a dollop of mango chutney on the side.

Vegan | Serves: 6 | Prep: 50 minutes | Cook: about 1 hour

400g (14oz) sweet potato, peeled and cut into 2cm (¾ inch) cubes

300g (10½oz) cauliflower, cut into small florets

1 tbsp vegetable oil

100g (3½oz) onion, finely chopped

2 garlic cloves, finely chopped

40g (1½oz) vegan tikka paste

200ml (7fl oz) coconut milk

200g (7oz) can chopped tomatoes

400g (14oz) can chickpeas, drained (keep the liquid to glaze the pies) and rinsed

100g (3½oz) fresh or frozen spinach

2–3 tbsp fresh chopped coriander

Salt

Pastry

300g (10½oz) plain flour, plus extra for dusting

150g (5½oz) dairy-free baking margarine, diced

2 tsp fennel or cumin seeds

Lightly steam the sweet potato and cauliflower for 5–10 minutes, until both are just tender.

Place a large saucepan over a medium heat and add the oil. When hot, add the onion and fry for 5 minutes. Add the garlic and cook for 2 minutes. Add the tikka paste, stir well and cook for two more minutes.

Add the coconut milk, chopped tomatoes, chickpeas, spinach and coriander and stir well. Bring to the boil and simmer for 10 minutes. Add the sweet potato and cauliflower and cook for a further 10 minutes. Season with salt to taste.

Preheat the oven to 190°C/180°C fan/gas 5.

To make the pastry, put the flour and margarine into a bowl and rub together until the mixture resembles fine crumbs. Add a pinch of salt and just enough cold water to bring the mixture together into a dough. On a lightly floured surface, roll out two-thirds of the pastry to 3mm (⅛ inch) thick and cut out six rounds, about 4cm (1½ inches) larger than your non-stick pie dishes. You can also use small 150–200ml (5–7fl oz) metal pudding moulds or deep muffin tins. Cut out six smaller rounds to make the pastry lids.

Gently press each of the larger rounds into a pie dish and fill with the vegetable mixture. Cover with the pastry lids. Brush with some of the reserved chickpea liquid and sprinkle with fennel or cumin seeds. Bake for 25–30 minutes until the pastry is golden and crisp.

Hunter's chicken

A simple, warming one-pot dinner. Serve with warm crusty bread, freshly cooked pasta or some mashed potato.

Serves: 4 | Prep: 20 minutes | Cook: 35–45 minutes

1 tbsp vegetable oil

100g (3½oz) smoked bacon, diced

200g (7oz) red onion, thinly sliced

1 garlic clove, roughly chopped

1 sprig of rosemary

500g (1lb 2oz) boneless, skinless chicken thighs, diced

3 tbsp dry white wine

400g (14oz) can chopped tomatoes

1½ tbsp tomato purée

250g (9oz) button mushrooms, halved

3 tbsp fresh chopped parsley

1 tsp dried oregano

1 bay leaf

Salt and pepper

Place a large saucepan over a high heat, add the oil, bacon and onion and fry for 8–10 minutes, stirring from time to time, until the bacon is golden brown.

Add the garlic, rosemary and chicken, reduce the heat to medium and fry for 5–7 minutes until the chicken is lightly browned all over.

Add the wine to the pan and stir to deglaze. Add the tomatoes, tomato purée, mushrooms, parsley, oregano and bay leaf. Stir well, bring to the boil, then reduce the heat, cover and simmer for 20–30 minutes until the chicken is cooked through.

Discard the rosemary and bay leaf, season to taste and serve hot.

Moroccan-style chicken stew

Roasting the tomatoes intensifies their flavour in this aromatic one-pot supper. It includes carrots and chickpeas, so all you need is something to mop up the sauce, such as crusty bread or couscous.

Serves: 4 | Prep: 45 minutes | Cook: 1 hour 15 minutes

300g (10½oz) tomatoes

1 tbsp vegetable oil

200g (7oz) onions, roughly chopped

500g (1lb 2oz) boneless, skinless chicken thighs, roughly chopped

2 garlic cloves, finely chopped

1 tsp ground cumin

1 tsp ground turmeric

1 tsp ground cinnamon

2 tbsp tomato purée

200g (7oz) carrots, peeled and roughly chopped

400ml (14fl oz) chicken stock

400g (14oz) can chickpeas, drained

20g (¾oz) flat-leaf parsley, finely chopped

50g (1¾oz) ready-to-eat dried apricots, roughly chopped

Salt and pepper

Preheat the oven to 190°C/180°C fan/gas 5 and line a roasting tin with non-stick baking paper.

Cut the tomatoes in half, and if they have hard, woody 'cores', cut these out with a small, sharp knife. Place the tomatoes cut-side down in the roasting tin and roast for 15–20 minutes, until they have softened and the skins have lifted away from the flesh. Remove the tomatoes from the oven and leave to cool slightly, then pinch off all the skins, saving any roasting juices.

Heat a large saucepan over a high heat; when hot, add the oil and the onions and fry for 10 minutes until softened.

Add the chicken, garlic, cumin, turmeric, cinnamon and tomato purée and cook, stirring, for 5 minutes.

Add the skinned roasted tomatoes and any roasting juices, the carrots, chicken stock and chickpeas and stir well. Reduce the heat and simmer for 20–30 minutes until the carrots have started to soften and the chicken is cooked through.

Stir in the parsley and dried apricots. Season to taste with salt and pepper.

Ratatouille with pistou

This Provençal dish is packed with the vibrant flavours of fresh summer vegetables and herbs. Serve hot or cold, as a starter, side dish or a light main course with warm, crusty bread.

Vegan | Serves: 4–6 | Prep: 40 minutes | Cook: 45 minutes

3 tbsp olive oil

1 aubergine, chopped
    into chunks

300g (10½oz) red
    onions, chopped

140g (5oz) fennel, chopped

300g (10½oz) fresh
    tomatoes

250g (9oz) red peppers,
    deseeded and chopped

250g (9oz) courgettes,
    chopped

1 large garlic clove,
    chopped

1 tbsp fresh thyme leaves

10g (⅓oz) fresh basil,
    roughly chopped

400g (14oz) can chopped
    tomatoes

4 tbsp boiling water

1 tsp caster sugar

Salt and pepper

Pistou

30g (1oz) fresh basil

30g (1oz) fresh parsley

30g (1oz) fresh mint

50g (1¾oz) fresh spinach

1 garlic clove, chopped

3–4 tbsp olive oil

Heat 1 tbsp of the oil in a large saucepan over a medium heat and fry the aubergine until it begins to colour. Transfer the aubergine to a large bowl using a slotted spoon.

Add another tablespoon of oil to the pan and fry the onions and fennel for 8–10 minutes until they begin to soften; remove and add to the bowl with the aubergine.

It's worth peeling and deseeding the fresh tomatoes for this dish. While the onions are softening, cut a small cross at the base of each tomato, place in a bowl and pour over boiling water to cover. Leave for about 10 seconds, then plunge into cold water: the skins should peel off easily. Cut the tomatoes in half around the equator and squeeze out the seeds, then cut into quarters.

Add another tablespoon of oil to the pan and fry the peppers, courgettes and garlic for 6–8 minutes until they begin to soften. Add them to the bowl with the other cooked vegetables, then add the quartered tomatoes, thyme, basil and canned tomatoes.

Return all the vegetables to the pan and stir in the boiling water and sugar. Bring to the boil and then reduce the heat, partly cover the pan, and simmer for 20–30 minutes until all the vegetables are tender.

To make the pistou, remove any tough stalks from the herbs and spinach, then place in a food processor with the garlic and olive oil and a pinch of salt and blitz until you have a thick sauce.

Season the ratatouille with salt and pepper to taste. Serve in bowls, with a generous spoonful of the pistou.

Chicken souvlaki with tzatziki

A taste of summer. These skewers are delicious when cooked outdoors, but even if your barbecue is rained off, you'll love this Mediterranean-style feast – perhaps with a glass of chilled rosé or sparkling water.

Serves: 4 | Prep: 20 minutes, plus marinating | Cook: 15 minutes

700g (1lb 9oz) boneless, skinless chicken thighs, cut into 3cm (1¼ inch) cubes

Marinade
2 tbsp olive oil
Grated zest and juice of 1 lemon
10g (⅓oz) fresh oregano, finely chopped, or 2 tsp dried oregano
1 tsp ground cumin
1 tsp ground coriander
1 garlic clove, finely chopped
2 tbsp dry white wine
Salt and pepper

Tzatziki
150g (5½oz) Greek-style natural yogurt
1 tbsp finely chopped fresh dill
1 tbsp finely chopped fresh oregano
1 garlic clove, finely chopped
2 tbsp extra-virgin olive oil

Mix all the marinade ingredients together in a bowl, add the chicken, cover and leave in the fridge to marinate for at least 1 hour, or overnight if possible.

To make the tzatziki, mix the yogurt, herbs and garlic in a bowl. Stir in 1 tbsp of the olive oil and season to taste. You can make this up to 24 hours in advance and keep it in the fridge.

Preheat the oven to 200°C/190°C fan/gas 6 or preheat the barbecue.

Thread the chicken cubes on to four large or eight small skewers. Cook in the oven or on the barbecue for 12–15 minutes, or until cooked through and beginning to brown.

Serve the chicken with flatbreads, lemon wedges and a Greek-style salad of chopped tomatoes, cucumbers, red onion and black olives. Transfer the tzatziki to a serving bowl and drizzle over the remaining olive oil.

Chicken, leek and tarragon pie

Crisp, golden pastry covers a creamy filling of chicken and vegetables in a sauce flavoured with tarragon – a classic partner for chicken. Serve with mashed potato and seasonal green veg.

Serves: 4 | Prep: 45 minutes | Cook: about 1 hour

Pastry
170g (6oz) plain flour,
    plus extra for dusting
85g (3oz) butter, diced
A pinch of salt
1 egg, beaten

Filling
1 tbsp vegetable oil
600g (1lb 5oz) boneless,
    skinless chicken
    thighs, diced
200g (7oz) leeks,
    thinly sliced
2 tbsp dry white wine
200g (7oz) carrots,
    peeled and diced
200g (7oz) squash or
    pumpkin, peeled,
    deseeded and diced
150ml (5fl oz) chicken
    stock
2 tbsp cornflour
4 tbsp double cream
2 tbsp fresh chopped
    parsley
2 tbsp fresh chopped
    tarragon
Salt and pepper

To make the pastry, put the flour, butter and salt into a bowl and rub together until it resembles fine crumbs. Mix in most of the egg (reserving a little to glaze) and about 1 tbsp cold water to bring the crumbs together to make a dough. Wrap in a clean, dry tea towel or beeswax wrap and leave to rest for 30 minutes.

To make the filling, place a large saucepan over a high heat and add the oil. When hot, add the chicken, leave for a couple of minutes, then stir and cook until the meat is lightly browned all over. Transfer the chicken to a plate using a slotted spoon.

Reduce the heat to medium, add the leeks to the pan and cook until they begin to soften. Pour in the wine and stir to deglaze the pan. Add the carrots and squash, stir well, then add the chicken stock and bring back to the boil. Return the chicken to the pan, cover and simmer for about 20 minutes or until the chicken is cooked through and the vegetables are tender.

Mix the cornflour with the cream and a ladleful of the hot stock from the pan; stir until smooth, then pour into the pan, stir well and simmer for 2–3 minutes. Add the parsley and tarragon, stir well and season to taste with salt and pepper. Leave to cool slightly, then spoon the mixture into a 1.2-litre (2-pint) pie dish.

Preheat the oven to 190°C/180°C fan/gas 5.

On a lightly floured surface, roll out the dough to about 3mm (⅛ inch) thick. Moisten the rim of the pie dish, lift the pastry over the dish and press into place. Trim off the excess pastry and crimp the edge. Brush with the remaining beaten egg and make a hole in the middle. Bake for 25–30 minutes, until the pastry is crisp and golden and the filling is hot when tested with a skewer.

Sticky sausages and polenta chips

A simple barbecue sauce transforms a sausage supper into something special. Serve with a crunchy slaw of shredded cabbage and carrot mixed with some chopped spring onions and lime mayo.

Serves: 4 | Prep: 20 minutes, plus chilling | Cook: 1 hour

8–12 pork sausages
(vegetarian/gluten-free
if preferred)

Polenta chips
800ml (28fl oz) water
1 vegetable stock cube,
   crumbled
200g (7oz) polenta
1 tbsp fresh chopped parsley
4–5 tbsp vegetable oil
Salt and pepper

Sticky barbecue sauce
1 tbsp light soy sauce
4 tbsp honey
1 tbsp toasted sesame oil
115g (4oz) tomato ketchup
1 tsp smoked paprika

COOK'S TIPS

Don't overcook the sauce
or it will become bitter.
   The polenta chips can
also be oven-baked: brush
them with a little oil
and place on the shelf
above the sausages for
25–30 minutes until crisp.

To make the polenta chips, line a baking tin, about 20cm (8 inches) square, with non-stick baking paper.

Bring the water to the boil in a heavy-based pan and stir in the stock cube. Pour in the polenta, whisking vigorously while the water comes back to the boil. Reduce the heat to a simmer, still whisking, for about 3 minutes, then reduce the heat to very low and simmer, stirring continuously, for a further 8–10 minutes until the polenta is thick and coming away from the side of the pan. Add the parsley and season to taste with salt and pepper. Pour into the lined tin and smooth over the surface, making sure it's even – it should be about 1.5cm (⅝ inch) thick. Leave to cool and then place in the fridge to chill for at least 2 hours until firm.

Preheat the oven to 200°C/190°C fan/gas 6.

To make the sauce, place all the ingredients in a saucepan and whisk until combined. Put the pan over a medium heat and bring to the boil. Reduce to a simmer and cook for 5 minutes until smooth and slightly thickened.

Place the sausages in a roasting tin and put into the oven for about 10 minutes, until just starting to colour. Remove from the oven and pour in the sauce, turn the sausages to coat them in sauce and return to the oven for a further 15–20 minutes, until cooked through.

Meanwhile, turn the chilled polenta out of the tin onto another sheet of baking paper and cut into 16 fingers. Heat the vegetable oil in a large frying pan over a high heat and fry the polenta chips for about 5 minutes, turning carefully until golden brown and crisp on all sides (or see Cook's Tips).

Serve the polenta chips with the sausages and a spoonful of the sauce.

Roasted cauliflower mac and cheese

This rich gratin is a satisfying supper dish, indulgent yet economical. Roasting intensifies the flavour of the cauliflower and avoids sogginess, and the crunchy topping adds the heavenly aroma of garlic bread.

Vegetarian | Serves: 4–6 | Prep: 30 minutes | Cook: 1 hour

1 cauliflower, about
   600g (1lb 5oz)
200g (7oz) macaroni
50g (1¾oz) butter
50g (1¾oz) plain flour
500ml (18fl oz) hot milk
170g (6oz) vegetarian
   Cheddar cheese, grated
Salt and pepper

Topping
100g (3½oz) bread, cut
   into small cubes
2 garlic cloves, finely
   chopped
20g (¾oz) parsley,
   finely chopped
1 tsp paprika
60g (2¼oz) vegetarian
   Cheddar cheese, grated

COOK'S TIPS

Use as much cauliflower as possible: chop the stalk and shred the leaves.

   This could also be made in individual ovenproof dishes.

Preheat the oven to 190°C/180°C fan/gas 5.

Cut the cauliflower into quarters, place on a baking sheet and roast for 20 minutes, then turn the pieces over and roast for a further 15–20 minutes until lightly coloured and just tender. Cut into florets and chop the stalk, discarding any very hard bits along with any burnt leaves (see Cook's Tips).

Meanwhile, cook the macaroni following the pack instructions. Drain and tip back into the pan.

Melt the butter in a saucepan over a medium heat, stir in the flour to make a smooth paste and cook for 1 minute, then gradually whisk in the milk and bring to the boil, whisking continuously for 5–6 minutes until the sauce is thickened and smooth. Remove from the heat, add the cheese and stir until the cheese has melted. Season to taste.

Add the macaroni to the cheese sauce and mix well. Place the cauliflower in a 1.7-litre (3-pint) ovenproof dish. Pour over the macaroni-cheese sauce and tap the dish on the work surface to settle the sauce.

To make the topping, put the bread cubes in a bowl, add the garlic, parsley, paprika and a pinch of salt and mix well. Add the cheese and mix again, then sprinkle over the sauce. Bake for about 20 minutes until the topping is golden and crisp and the centre is piping hot (test with a skewer).

Honey-roast squash, pearl barley and kale

Showcasing seasonal squash or pumpkin in two ways – added to a creamy pearl barley risotto, and oven-roasted – this dish is topped with kale and a scattering of nuts and seeds for a really healthy meal.

Vegetarian | Serves: 4 | Prep: 40 minutes | Cook: about 1 hour

Squash and tomato pearl barley risotto

1 tbsp olive oil or oil from the sun-dried tomatoes

1 red onion, finely chopped

2 garlic cloves, finely chopped

170g (6oz) pearl barley, rinsed

200g (7oz) carrots, peeled and diced

About 1 litre (1¾ pints) hot vegetable stock

300g (10½oz) butternut squash, peeled, deseeded and diced

40g (1½oz) drained weight sun-dried tomatoes, sliced

1 tsp tomato purée

4 tbsp dry white wine

1 tsp white wine vinegar

2 tbsp fresh chopped parsley

4 tbsp double cream

To make the risotto, heat the oil in a large, deep frying pan over a low heat, add the onion and garlic and fry for 2–3 minutes until they begin to soften. Add the pearl barley and stir until coated in the oil. Increase the heat, add the carrots and about 300ml (½ pint) of the hot stock and bring to the boil. Reduce the heat, cover and simmer for about 20 minutes, stirring frequently and adding more stock if needed to prevent the barley from sticking.

Add the squash, tomatoes, tomato purée, white wine, vinegar and another 300ml (½ pint) stock. Stir well and simmer for a further 20 minutes, adding more hot stock (or just-boiled water) if needed, until the barley is soft and the risotto is rich and thick.

While the risotto is cooking, make the honey-roast squash. Preheat the oven to 180°C/170°C fan/gas 4 and line a large baking sheet with non-stick baking paper. Place the squash wedges on the baking sheet, drizzle over the oil and season with salt and pepper. Roast for about 25 minutes until just tender. Drizzle over the honey and return to the oven for 5 minutes. Remove from the oven and keep warm.

Honey-roast squash

1kg (2lb 3oz) butternut
squash, peeled, deseeded
and cut into wedges
about 1cm (½ inch) thick
2 tbsp cold-pressed
rapeseed oil
1½ tbsp honey
Salt and pepper

Dressing

4 tbsp cold-pressed
rapeseed oil
1 tbsp honey
1 tbsp white wine vinegar
1 tbsp fresh chopped
chives

To finish

170g (6oz) kale, roughly
chopped
115g (4oz) full-fat soft
cheese, cut into
small pieces
30g (1oz) walnuts,
lightly crushed
2 tbsp sunflower seeds
3 tbsp pumpkin seeds

Meanwhile, blanch the kale until soft. Drain, rinse in cold water and drain well. Set aside.

Whisk all the dressing ingredients together in a bowl.

To finish, heat a little oil over a high heat in a large frying pan, add the kale and cook until hot.

Add the chopped parsley to the risotto and stir well, then add the cream and season to taste. Divide the risotto between four serving plates. Add the kale, then the wedges of roasted squash. Dot the cheese over the squash, scatter the nuts and seeds on top and drizzle over the dressing.

Mushroom suet puddings

Of course, we can get mushrooms all year round, but this hearty veggie recipe highlights their autumnal character. Serve with green vegetables, such as buttered cabbage.

Vegetarian | **Serves: 4** | **Prep: 30 minutes** | **Cook: 1 hour 15 minutes**

30g (1oz) dried mushrooms

30g (1oz) butter, plus extra
    for greasing

1 tbsp vegetable oil

300g (10½oz) onions,
    finely sliced

2 garlic cloves, finely
    chopped

300g (10½oz) mushrooms,
    roughly chopped

2 tbsp dry white wine

2 tbsp finely chopped
    fresh parsley

1 tbsp finely chopped
    fresh sage

2 tbsp double cream

Salt and pepper

Suet pastry

340g (12oz) self-raising
    flour, plus extra
    for dusting

170g (6oz) vegetarian suet

175–200ml (6–7fl oz) water

Put the dried mushrooms in a bowl and add enough boiling water to cover them. Cover the bowl and leave to soak for at least 30 minutes. Drain the mushrooms, reserving the soaking liquid, and roughly chop.

Heat the butter and oil in a large saucepan over a medium heat. Add the onions and fry for about 5 minutes until beginning to soften. Then add the garlic, chopped mushrooms and soaked mushrooms, stir well and fry for 5–10 minutes.

Increase the heat and add the wine. Add enough of the reserved mushroom soaking liquid to make a thin sauce (keep any remaining liquid to make the gravy), then stir in the herbs and cream. Season to taste with salt and pepper. Remove from the heat and set aside.

To make the pastry, put the flour, suet, and a good pinch of salt and pepper in a bowl and stir together. Gradually mix in enough water to make a soft but not sticky dough. Lightly knead on a floured surface and then cut into four pieces. Cut off a quarter of each piece of dough and reserve to make the lids.

Roll out one of the larger pieces of dough to make a circle about 18cm (7 inches) in diameter – about 3mm (⅛ inch thick) – and then press the dough into a lightly buttered 250ml (9fl oz) pudding basin or metal pudding mould, leaving the pastry overhanging the rim. Repeat to fill three more basins.

Mushroom gravy

½ tbsp vegetable oil

1 shallot or small onion,
    finely chopped

50g (1¾oz) mushrooms,
    finely chopped

1 tbsp plain flour

300ml (½ pint) hot
    vegetable stock or
    just-boiled water

2 tbsp double cream

COOK'S TIP

If you don't have a
steamer, put the puddings
in a roasting tin, pour
boiling water into the
tin to come halfway up
the sides of the pudding
moulds, then cover the
tin with foil and seal well
around the tin's edges.
Bake in a preheated oven
at 180°C/170°C fan/gas 4
for about 1 hour.

Spoon in the mushroom mixture, filling to around 1cm (½ inch) from the top of the container.

Roll out the smaller pieces of dough to make lids for the puddings. Moisten the edges of the pastry in the basins with water and press the lids in place, folding over the overhanging pastry and trimming off any excess. Cover the tops of the puddings with buttered foil, doming the foil slightly to allow for the pastry to rise. Put the puddings into a large steamer set over a saucepan of simmering water (or see Cook's Tip). Cover and steam for about 1 hour until the pastry is risen and firm.

To make the gravy, heat the oil in a small saucepan over a medium heat, add the shallot and mushrooms and fry for 8–10 minutes until softened and golden brown. Sprinkle over the flour, stirring continuously, and cook for about a minute. Stir in the stock or water and any leftover liquid from soaking the mushrooms, then stir in the cream and simmer until slightly thickened. Season to taste and pour through a sieve into a warmed jug.

Use an oven glove or doubled tea towel to lift the puddings out of the steamer. Remove the foil and turn out on to warmed plates. Serve with a generous helping of mushroom gravy.

Chilli non carne

*This vegan chilli is packed with flavour and is guaranteed to warm you up
on a chilly day. Serve with rice, crusty bread or tortillas.*

Vegan | Serves: 4 | Prep: 1 hour | Cook: 1 hour

Spice mix

1 tsp chilli powder

2½ tsp ground cumin

3 tsp ground coriander

2 tsp smoked paprika

1 tsp dried oregano

¼–½ tsp dried chilli flakes

2 tsp cocoa powder

Base

1 small onion

1 red pepper

2 garlic cloves

1 tsp rapeseed oil

2 tbsp fresh coriander

Chilli

1 small yellow pepper

½ green pepper

150g (5½oz) mushrooms

100g (3½oz) split red lentils

3 tbsp vegan red wine

3 tbsp tomato purée

400g (14oz) can chopped
    tomatoes

1 tsp white wine vinegar

200ml (7fl oz) vegetable stock

400g (14oz) can red kidney
    beans

2 tbsp fresh coriander

Salt and pepper

To make the spice mix, put all the spices and the cocoa into a bowl, add 3 tbsp of water and stir until they form a paste. Set aside.

To make the base, roughly chop the onion and deseed and roughly chop the red pepper. Peel the garlic. Put the onion, red pepper, garlic, oil and coriander into a food processor and blitz until finely chopped.

Place a large saucepan over a high heat and, when hot, add the base mixture. When the mixture starts to sizzle, reduce the heat to low and cook for about 10 minutes until it starts to dry out and is lightly colouring.

Add the spice mix, stir through and cook for 5 minutes.

To make the chilli, deseed the peppers and roughly chop. Finely chop the mushrooms. Rinse the red lentils. Add the peppers, mushrooms and lentils to the spiced base mixture, then add the wine, tomato purée, chopped tomatoes, white wine vinegar and stock, stir well and gently simmer for 15 minutes.

Drain the kidney beans and add to the pan, season with salt and pepper and stir well. Bring to the boil, then reduce the heat and simmer, uncovered, for 30 minutes.

Stir through the fresh chopped coriander and serve hot, in bowls.

Nut roast

This very nutty nut loaf, studded with cranberries, is a vegetarian treat at any time of year. Serve with all your favourite Christmas trimmings, or simply with cooked cabbage and carrots.

Vegetarian | Serves: 6–8 | Prep: 30 minutes | Cook: about 1 hour 15 minutes

1 tbsp vegetable oil

300g (10½oz) onions, finely chopped

2 garlic cloves, crushed

300g (10½oz) mushrooms: half sliced, half finely chopped

1 tbsp mixed dried herbs

2 tbsp red wine

4 eggs

150g (5½oz) cottage cheese

300g (10½oz) mixed nuts, finely chopped

70g (2½oz) cooked long-grain rice

20g (¾oz) fresh parsley, finely chopped

70g (2½oz) dried cranberries

200g (7oz) vegetarian Cheddar cheese, grated

Salt and pepper

COOK'S TIP

Using a food processor makes it easy to chop the nuts: do this first and set aside, then use the processor to chop the mushrooms, onions and garlic.

Preheat the oven to 190°C/180°C fan/gas 5. Line a 900g (2lb) loaf tin with non-stick baking paper.

Heat the oil in a large saucepan over a low–medium heat, add the onions and garlic and fry for 8–10 minutes, stirring occasionally, until the onions are soft.

Add the sliced mushrooms and fry for 3–4 minutes until they start to colour and release some of their liquid. Increase the heat, add the finely chopped mushrooms and dried herbs and cook for 4–5 minutes until the mixture starts to dry out. Add the red wine, salt and pepper and stir to deglaze the pan. Remove from the heat.

While the mushroom mixture is cooling, combine the eggs and cottage cheese in a large bowl. Add the chopped nuts, the cooked rice and the parsley and mix well. Finally, add the mushroom mixture, cranberries and grated cheese and mix well.

Spoon the mixture into the loaf tin, level the top with a spatula and give the tin a couple of taps on the work surface to remove any air bubbles. Bake for about 50 minutes–1 hour or until firm. A skewer inserted into the centre of the loaf for 5–10 seconds should come out piping hot.

Leave in the tin for 10–15 minutes before turning out on to a serving plate and slicing into portions.

Game and celeriac stew

A tasty one-pot supper. Serve with creamy mashed potatoes or warm bread.

Serves: 4 | Prep: 25 minutes | Cook: about 2 hours 30 minutes

2 tbsp vegetable oil

200g (7oz) game mix,
    such as pheasant,
    pigeon or rabbit

200g (7oz) diced venison

50g (1¾oz) bacon, finely
    diced

1 onion, roughly chopped

150g (5½oz) carrots, peeled
    and sliced about 1cm
    (½ inch) thick

150g (5½oz) swede, peeled
    and cut into 2–3cm
    (about 1 inch) chunks

200g (7oz) celeriac, peeled
    and cut into 2–3cm
    (about 1 inch) chunks

2 garlic cloves, crushed

5 juniper berries

A small pinch of ground
    cloves, or 2 whole cloves

1 bay leaf

75ml (5 tbsp) red wine

1 tbsp tomato purée

50g (1¾oz) pitted prunes

400ml (14fl oz) chicken
    stock

1 tbsp cornflour

Salt and pepper

Heat half the oil in a flameproof casserole dish over a high heat, add the game and venison and fry – in batches, if needed, to avoid overcrowding the pan – until browned all over. Scoop the meat out of the pan using a slotted spoon and set aside.

Add the remaining oil to the pan and fry the bacon and onion for about 5 minutes, stirring from time to time, until golden.

Add the vegetables, garlic, juniper berries, cloves, bay leaf, wine, tomato purée and prunes, season with salt and pepper and stir well. Return the meat to the pan. Add just enough of the stock to cover, bring to the boil and then reduce to a very gentle simmer. Cover and cook for 1½–2 hours until the meat is tender.

Mix the cornflour with a little water until smooth and stir into the stew. Bring back to the boil and simmer for a couple of minutes until thickened. Taste and adjust the seasoning. Serve hot, in bowls.

Ham, leek and Cheddar crumble

A creamy, comforting savoury crumble, ideal for making a wonderful new dish from leftover boiled or baked ham. Serve with a side dish of buttered shredded cabbage or other seasonal greens.

Serves: 4 | Prep: 30 minutes | Cook: 45 minutes

150g (5½oz) potatoes, peeled and diced

1 tbsp butter

1 onion, finely chopped

340g (12oz) leeks, cut into 2cm (¾ inch) slices

1 garlic clove, finely chopped

100g (3½oz) button mushrooms, sliced

2 tbsp dry white wine

30g (1oz) plain flour

200ml (7fl oz) hot chicken stock

2 tbsp double cream

1 tsp wholegrain mustard

50g (1¾oz) Cheddar cheese, grated

340g (12oz) cooked ham, diced or shredded

2 tbsp fresh chopped parsley

Salt and pepper

Crumble topping

150g (5½oz) wholemeal flour

70g (2½oz) butter, cubed

30g (1oz) Cheddar cheese, grated

½ tsp dried mixed herbs

Preheat the oven to 180°C/170°C fan/gas 4. Boil or steam the diced potatoes for 5–7 minutes until tender, drain and set aside.

Heat the butter in a large, heavy-based saucepan, add the onion and leeks and fry over a medium heat for 8–10 minutes until softened but not coloured. Add the garlic and mushrooms and cook for 4–5 minutes. Add the wine, turn up the heat and stir to deglaze the pan.

Once the wine has almost evaporated, sprinkle the flour over the vegetables and cook, stirring, for 2–3 minutes. Gradually add the chicken stock, stirring until the sauce thickens. Remove from the heat and stir in the cream, mustard, cheese, ham, potatoes and parsley. Season to taste.

To make the crumble topping, put the flour and butter into a mixing bowl and rub together until the mixture resembles fine crumbs. Add the cheese and herbs, season with freshly ground black pepper and mix well.

Spoon the ham mixture into a 1.2-litre (2-pint) ovenproof dish, top with the crumble and bake for 20–25 minutes until golden.

Sausage and fennel-seed pasta

A quick, simple and versatile all-in-one supper dish that can be adapted to use whatever pasta and spices you have in the cupboard.

Serves: 2 | Prep: 15 minutes | Cook: 25–30 minutes

3 pork sausages

½ tsp fennel seeds

¼ tsp dried chilli flakes

¼ tsp salt

¼ tsp pepper

1 tbsp olive oil

140g (5oz) linguine (or pasta of your choice)

100g (3½oz) fresh young spinach, washed

Grated Parmesan or Cheddar cheese (optional), to serve

Remove the skins from the sausages and place the sausage meat in a bowl. Add the fennel seeds, chilli flakes, salt and pepper and mix together until thoroughly combined.

Heat the olive oil in a frying pan over a medium heat. Using a teaspoon, carefully place pieces of the sausage meat into the pan and fry for about 15 minutes until crisp, caramelised and cooked through, turning regularly.

Meanwhile, cook the pasta according to the pack instructions until just tender. Drain, reserving 2 tbsp of the cooking water. Add the spinach and the cooked pasta to the pan with the sausage meat, along with the reserved pasta water, and stir until the spinach has wilted.

Divide between two serving bowls, and top with a little grated cheese if liked.

COOK'S TIPS

Try this with vegetarian, vegan or gluten-free sausages if you prefer.

If you have a courgette in the fridge, grate it and add at the same time as the spinach.

Instead of the fennel seeds and chilli flakes, stir in 1 tbsp pesto, harissa or chipotle paste.

Slow-roast spiced shoulder of lamb

For a relaxed feast for family and friends, serve the lamb on a platter in the middle of the table, with breads and salads to pass round.

Serves: 4–6 | Prep: 30 minutes | Cook: 2–3 hours

1½ tbsp ground cumin

2 tbsp ground coriander

1 tbsp smoked paprika

3 tbsp finely chopped fresh
   rosemary leaves

5 garlic cloves, chopped

4 tbsp olive oil

1 lamb shoulder, about
   1.8–2kg (4–4½lb)

Salt and pepper

Mint yogurt

400g (14oz) yogurt

15g (½oz) fresh mint,
   finely chopped

Red-cabbage salad

1 red onion, thinly sliced

200g (7oz) red cabbage,
   thinly shredded

3 tbsp white wine vinegar

Flatbreads

200g (7oz) self-raising flour,
   plus extra for dusting

200g (7oz) Greek-style
   natural yogurt

1–2 tsp nigella seeds, or
   roughly crushed cumin
   or fennel seeds (optional)

Preheat the oven to 160°C/150°C fan/gas 3.

In a small bowl, mix the cumin, coriander, smoked paprika and rosemary with some salt and pepper until evenly combined. Mix in the garlic and oil.

Place the lamb shoulder on a large sheet of foil, add the spice mix and rub in to coat the meat. Wrap the lamb in the foil, sealing well, place in a roasting tin and cook for 2–3 hours or until very tender. Remove from the oven and leave to rest.

While the lamb is in the oven, make the mint yogurt and red-cabbage salad. Put the yogurt in a bowl and mix in the mint. Put the red onion and red cabbage in another bowl, add the vinegar, season to taste and mix well. Set aside.

While the lamb is resting, put the flour, yogurt, seeds (if using), and a pinch of salt in a bowl and mix until you have a soft but not sticky dough. Divide into four or six pieces. On a well-floured surface, roll out each piece to an oval shape about 3mm (⅛ inch) thick. Heat a dry frying pan until very hot. Add the breads one at a time and cook for 2–3 minutes until they begin to brown underneath, then turn and cook the other side. Keep them warm while you cook the remaining flatbreads.

Shred the lamb or carve into thin slices and lay out on a large serving plate. Serve the warm flatbreads, mint yogurt and red cabbage separately for people to help themselves.

Beef, ale and horseradish cobbler

Beef braised slowly in ale and topped with horseradish scones is just the sort of hearty dish you'll look forward to after a brisk winter walk.

Serves: 6 | Prep: 25 minutes | Cook: about 2 hours

2 tbsp vegetable oil

600g (1lb 5oz) stewing
    steak, diced

2 onions, chopped

3 sticks of celery, chopped

A good pinch of grated
    nutmeg

200g (7oz) butternut
    squash, peeled, deseeded
    and chopped

150g (5½oz) mushrooms,
    roughly chopped

250ml (9fl oz) ale

200g (7oz) can chopped
    tomatoes

About 250ml (9fl oz)
    beef stock

2 tbsp cornflour

Salt and pepper

1 tbsp fresh chopped
    parsley, to garnish

Scone topping

200g (7oz) self-raising
    flour, plus extra
    for dusting

55g (2oz) butter, diced

2 tbsp horseradish sauce

1 egg, beaten

A splash of milk

Preheat the oven to 160°C/150°C fan/gas 3.

Heat 1 tbsp of the oil in a wide, flameproof casserole over a high heat, add the steak and fry – in batches, if needed, to avoid overcrowding the pan – for about 5 minutes until browned all over. Transfer to a plate using a slotted spoon.

Reduce the heat and, if needed, add a little more oil to the pan, then add the onions and celery and fry for about 5 minutes, stirring from time to time, until softened. Stir in the nutmeg, then add the butternut squash and mushrooms; stir well and fry for a further 3–4 minutes.

Return the meat to the pan. Pour in the ale and add the tomatoes and enough beef stock to cover the meat. Season with salt and pepper, bring to the boil, then cover with a lid and place in the oven for about 1½ hours or until the meat is tender. (Alternatively, cook on the hob over a very low heat for about 1½ hours.)

Mix the cornflour with a little water, until smooth, and stir into the stew. Bring back to the boil and simmer for a couple of minutes until thickened. Taste and adjust the seasoning. Return the stew to the oven while you make the topping.

Turn up the oven to 200°C/190°C fan/gas 6. To make the scone topping, sift the flour into a mixing bowl and add the butter and a pinch of salt and pepper. Using your fingertips, rub the butter into the flour until the mixture resembles fine crumbs. Make a well in the centre and add the horseradish and the egg. Mix with the dry ingredients, adding a little milk until you have a soft dough. Tip the dough on to a lightly floured surface and gently press it down to flatten it. Use a small, 3–4cm (about 1½ inch), cutter to cut out 12 scones. Arrange the scones on top of the stew, leaving enough room for them to rise. Lightly brush the tops with milk, then bake for 10–15 minutes until risen and golden. Garnish with parsley and serve immediately.

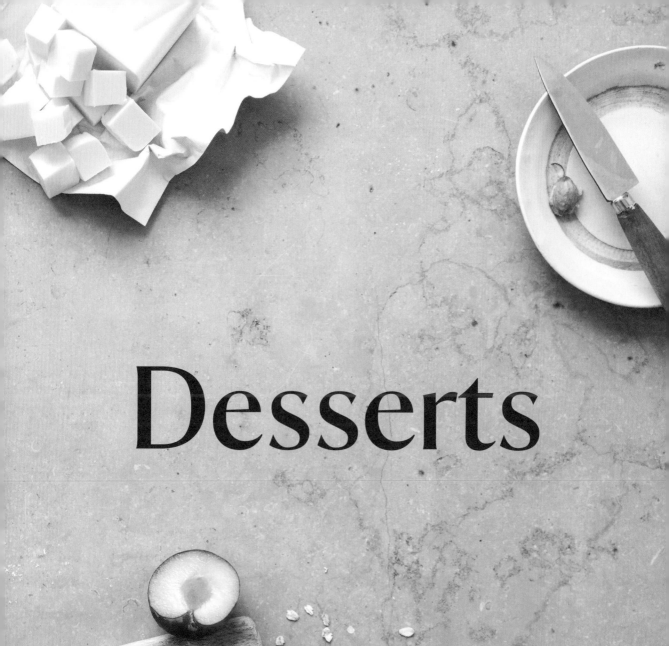

Desserts

Blueberry and lemon mousse pot

This dainty, rich yet tangy dessert is easy to make and it's a great way to use blueberries.

Serves: 4 | **Prep: 20 minutes, plus chilling** | **Cook: 10 minutes**

Blueberry compote

150g (5½oz) blueberries

20g (¾oz) caster sugar

1 tbsp water

To make the compote, put the blueberries, sugar and water in a saucepan over a low heat and bring to a simmer until the blueberries start to release their juices and the sugar has dissolved. Divide between four small glass serving dishes and chill until cold.

Lemon mousse

150g (5½oz) lemon curd

Grated zest and juice
   of 1 lemon

200ml (7fl oz) double
   cream

To make the mousse, put the lemon curd in a bowl and add the lemon zest and juice. Beat until smooth.

Whip the cream in a bowl until it forms soft peaks. Add the lemon curd and gently fold through – it's fine if some swirls of lemon curd remain. Gently spoon the mousse over the blueberry compote and tap the dishes once or twice to settle the mixture. Place in the fridge to chill for at least 45 minutes.

To serve

50g (1¾oz) blueberries

Serve with fresh blueberries on top.

COOK'S TIPS

Prepare up to 24 hours ahead and keep covered in the fridge.

You can use frozen blueberries instead of fresh: make the compote with 200g (7oz) frozen berries; set aside 4 teaspoons of the compote to serve on top of the mousse.

Baked rhubarb and ginger cheesecake

Luscious creamy cheesecake with a zingy rhubarb and ginger topping. Early 'forced' rhubarb gives a vibrant pink colour but outdoor-grown tastes just as good.

Serves: 10–12 | Prep: 30 minutes, plus chilling | Cook: about 1 hour

Base

250g (9oz) digestive biscuits

55g (2oz) caster sugar

2 tsp ground ginger

125g (4½oz) butter, melted

Filling

500g (1lb 2oz) cream cheese

150g (5½oz) caster sugar

4 tbsp cornflour

Grated zest and juice
of 1 lemon

4 eggs

200g (7oz) natural yogurt

Topping

4 tbsp stem ginger syrup

400g (14oz) trimmed
rhubarb, cut into
2cm (¾ inch) pieces

50g (1¾oz) stem ginger,
thinly sliced

COOK'S TIP

Place a small metal bowl of water in the bottom of the oven while baking the cheesecake: this helps to prevent cracking.

Preheat the oven to 180°C/170°C fan/gas 4. Lightly oil a 23cm (9 inch) springform tin and line the base with non-stick baking paper.

Blitz the biscuits in a food processor, or place them in a bowl and crush with the end of a rolling pin until they form fine crumbs. Tip into a bowl, add the sugar and ground ginger and mix well. Add the melted butter and mix until evenly combined. Press the crumb mixture into the base of the lined tin, using the back of a spoon to get an even layer.

Bake for 5 minutes, then remove from the oven and set aside to cool. Turn the oven down to 160°C/150°C fan/gas 3.

To make the filling, put the cream cheese, caster sugar and cornflour into a bowl and whisk together until smooth. Add the lemon zest and juice, eggs and yogurt and whisk again until smooth.

Pour the filling into the tin and bake for 45 minutes–1 hour until set on the top with a slight wobble in the centre (see Cook's Tip). Remove from the oven and leave to cool in the tin. Chill in the fridge for 2–3 hours.

For the topping, put the stem-ginger syrup into a large pan with 2 tbsp water and bring to the boil. Add the rhubarb and the sliced ginger and simmer for a couple of minutes until the rhubarb begins to soften slightly (it will soften further as it chills). Tip into a bowl and leave to cool, then chill in the fridge.

Spoon the rhubarb mixture over the top of the cheesecake. Chill until ready to serve. To serve, run a thin, flexible knife around the outside of the cheesecake to loosen it, then unclip the tin and slide the cheesecake onto a serving plate.

Bread pudding

With its crisp top and moist middle, this dessert is a classic way to use up leftover bread or buns. It's quick and easy to prepare and will happily sit in the oven while you eat your main course.

Serves: 4–6 | Prep: 10 minutes | Cook: 40–45 minutes

250g (9oz) leftover
    bread, currant buns
    or Chelsea buns
85g (3oz) sultanas
1 egg
250ml (9fl oz) milk
100g (3½oz) soft
    brown sugar
2 tsp ground mixed spice
1 tbsp demerara sugar

Preheat the oven to 180°C/170°C fan/gas 4. Line a 450g (1lb) loaf tin with non-stick baking paper.

Rip the bread into small pieces and place in a large bowl with the sultanas.

Mix the egg, milk, soft brown sugar and mixed spice together and pour over the bread. Scrunch the bread in the milk mixture until all the liquid has soaked in. Tip into the lined loaf tin and sprinkle over the demerara sugar. Bake for 40–45 minutes until the top is golden and the pudding is just set.

Leave to firm up for about 15 minutes before serving with custard, or leave to cool completely, slice and serve as a cake with a cup of tea.

COOK'S TIP

If you use leftover buns, you may need less sugar or fewer sultanas.

Peach frangipane tart

Peaches and nectarines can grow well in Britain if they're planted in a sunny, sheltered spot. For this dessert you'll need fragrant, ripe, juicy fruit – or use well-drained canned peaches.

Serves: 10 | Prep: 30 minutes, plus chilling | Cook: about 1 hour 15 minutes

Wholemeal pastry

125g (4½oz) wholemeal
    plain flour
125g (4½oz) plain flour
125g (4½oz) butter
A pinch of salt
30g (1oz) icing sugar,
    plus extra for dusting
1 egg, beaten
1 tbsp milk

Filling

150g (5½oz) caster sugar
125g (4½oz) butter, softened
2 eggs, beaten
125g (4½oz) ground almonds
125g (4½oz) ground rice
½ tsp almond essence
5 ripe peaches, halved,
    stones removed

COOK'S TIP

You can use canned peach halves instead of fresh, but make sure they are drained and patted dry. You will need 2 x 400g (14oz) cans (each can contains about 6 halves).

To make the pastry, put the flours, butter, salt and icing sugar in a food processor and blitz until the mixture resembles fine crumbs. Add the egg and milk and pulse until the mixture starts to form a ball. Tip on to a lightly floured surface and knead a couple of times to bring the pastry together.

Roll out the pastry and use to line a loose-bottomed, deep, 23cm (9 inch) tart tin. Prick the base all over with a fork and chill for 15–30 minutes.

Preheat the oven to 190°C/180°C fan/gas 5.

Line the pastry case with a circle of non-stick baking paper, then fill with baking beans. Put the tin on a baking sheet and bake for 10–15 minutes. Remove the paper and beans and cook for about 5 more minutes until the pastry is crisp and dry.

To make the filling, put the caster sugar and butter in a food processor and blitz until light and fluffy. Add the remaining ingredients, except the peaches, and pulse until combined. Spoon into the pastry case and spread evenly.

Place the peaches, cut-sides down, around the edge of the tart, pressing gently into the frangipane filling. Place them close together as they will shrink during cooking.

Turn the oven down to 180°C/170°C fan/gas 4 and bake for 40–55 minutes or until the top is golden brown and the filling is set but with a little wobble in the centre. Remove from the oven and leave to cool.

Sift a little icing sugar over the tart before serving.

Lavender and honey panna cotta

This silky, creamy dessert captures the essence of a warm summer day in the garden. Serve with ripe, fresh strawberries, or this quick strawberry compote and a drizzle of honey.

Serves: 4 | Prep: 15 minutes, plus chilling | Cook: 10 minutes

2 sheets of gelatine

300ml (½ pint) double cream

120ml (4fl oz) milk

3 sprigs of lavender or 1–2 tsp dried lavender flowers

1 tsp vanilla extract

60g (2¼oz) honey, plus extra to serve

Strawberry compote

200g (7oz) strawberries, hulled and chopped

2 tbsp strawberry jam

COOK'S TIPS

If using fresh lavender, wash it in a little salted water to draw out any bugs.

If using dried lavender, the amount may depend on how fragrant the lavender is. Remember that cold tends to dull flavours, but on the other hand don't go over the top!

Put the gelatine in a shallow dish, cover with cold water and leave to soften for 5 minutes.

Warm the cream, milk, lavender and vanilla in a saucepan over a low heat and slowly bring to a simmer. Reduce the heat and leave the pan on the hob for 5 minutes, squeezing the lavender flowers from time to time to extract as much flavour as possible. Turn off the heat and stir through the honey.

Remove the gelatine from the water and squeeze to remove excess water. Add to the warm cream mixture and stir until the gelatine has completely dissolved.

Strain the cream mixture through a sieve into a jug, then divide between four 150ml (5fl oz) pudding moulds. Leave to cool, then place in the fridge and leave to set for at least 4 hours, or overnight.

To make the compote, mix the chopped strawberries and strawberry jam together in a bowl.

To serve, dip each mould, one at a time, into a bowl of just-boiled water, count to four, remove from the water, and then gently loosen around the edges of the panna cotta with a fingertip and turn out on to a serving plate. Spoon over a portion of the compote and drizzle over a little honey.

Summer berry tart

Raspberries, loganberries, strawberries, blueberries – all work well atop this colourful tart with an easy-to-make, rich and citrussy filling.

Serves: 10 | Prep: 30 minutes, plus chilling | Cook: about 1 hour

Sweet pastry
250g (9oz) plain flour
125g (4½oz) butter
50g (1¾oz) icing sugar,
    plus extra for dusting
1 egg, beaten
Grated zest and juice
    of ½ lemon

Filling
250g (9oz) Greek-style
    yogurt
400g (14oz) can condensed
    milk
4 eggs
Grated zest and juice
    of 2 limes

Topping
50g (1¾oz) Greek-style
    yogurt
250g (9oz) seasonal berries

To make the pastry, put the flour, butter and icing sugar in a food processor and blitz until the mixture resembles fine crumbs. Add the egg, lemon zest and juice and pulse a few times to bring the pastry together.

On a lightly floured surface, roll out the pastry and use to line a loose-bottomed, deep, 23cm (9 inch) tart tin. Prick the base all over with a fork and chill for 15–30 minutes.

Preheat the oven to 190°C/180°C fan/gas 5.

Line the pastry case with a circle of non-stick baking paper, then fill with baking beans. Put the tin on a baking sheet and bake for 10–15 minutes. Remove the paper and beans and cook for about 5 more minutes until the pastry is crisp and dry.

To make the filling, put the yogurt, condensed milk, eggs, lime zest and juice in a bowl and beat until smooth.

Turn the oven down to 160°C/150°C fan/gas 3. Pour the filling into the pastry case (still on the baking sheet) and bake for 35–40 minutes or until the filling is just set, with a slight wobble, and lightly coloured on top. Remove from the oven and leave to cool.

For the topping, spread the yogurt over the filling. Scatter the berries over the yogurt. Sift a little icing sugar over the berries to serve.

Poached pears

The orange-flavoured syrup is lightly spiced with star anise in this variation on a classic dessert. Serve it warm or make ahead and chill – either way, it's delicious.

Vegan | Serves: 6 | Prep: 15 minutes | Cook: 20–30 minutes

200ml (7fl oz) vegan
    white wine
2½ tbsp maple syrup
6 star anise
1 cinnamon stick, broken
    in half, or 1 tsp ground
    cinnamon
4 cloves
2 oranges
6 pears
Caster sugar (optional)

Put the wine, maple syrup, star anise, cinnamon and cloves into a saucepan just large enough to hold all the pears, standing upright. Using a potato peeler or citrus zester, cut thin strips of orange peel and add to the pan. Squeeze the oranges, then add the juice and squeezed fruit to the pan.

Peel the pears, then cut a little slice off the bottom of each pear so they stand upright. Stand the pears in the pan and add just enough water to cover them two-thirds of the way up. Bring to the boil and then immediately reduce to a simmer. Cover the pan and poach for about 20 minutes. Test the pears by pushing a small, pointed knife into the widest part: it should slide in easily. Remove the pears from the poaching liquid and set aside. To serve cold, place in the fridge to chill.

Increase the heat and boil the liquid until it has reduced by half and thickened slightly. Taste and add sugar if needed. Strain into a bowl; if you like, you can reserve the orange peel and star anise to decorate. To serve cold, place the syrup in the fridge to chill for at least 2 hours.

Place each pear in a serving bowl and ladle over some of the poaching liquid. If using, decorate with a star anise and a few strands of the orange peel. For added indulgence, serve with dairy-free cream or ice cream.

COOK'S TIP

When poaching the pears, make sure the liquid is simmering and not boiling, otherwise the pears will disintegrate.

Apple and pear pie with caramel sauce

A spicy autumnal pie with a rich, vegan-friendly caramel sauce. It's a great way to use windfall or slightly imperfect apples and pears.

Vegan | Serves: 4–6 | Prep: 30 minutes, plus chilling | Cook: 30 minutes

Pastry
170g (6oz) plain flour,
   plus extra for dusting
85g (3oz) dairy-free
   baking margarine
30g (1oz) icing sugar
A pinch of salt

Filling
300g (10½oz) Bramley
   apples, peeled, cored
   and chopped
300g (10½oz) pears, peeled,
   cored and chopped
60g (2¼oz) caster sugar
Grated zest and juice
   of ½ lime
½ tsp ground cinnamon
½ tsp ground ginger
A pinch of grated nutmeg
A pinch of ground cloves

Caramel sauce
125g (4½oz) caster sugar
200ml (7fl oz) coconut
   milk

To make the pastry, put the flour, margarine, icing sugar and salt in a food processor and blitz until the mixture resembles fine crumbs. Add a little water and pulse until the pastry comes together. Wrap in a clean, dry tea towel or beeswax wrap and chill for 20–30 minutes.

To make the filling, put all the ingredients in a large bowl and mix together well. Tip the fruit mixture into a 1.2-litre (2-pint) pie dish.

Preheat the oven to 200°C/190°C fan/gas 6.

On a lightly floured surface, roll out the pastry and cut out a piece slightly bigger than the pie dish. Place the pastry on top of the fruit and crimp the edges against the side of the dish. With a sharp knife, make a small hole in the top. Bake for 20–25 minutes until the pastry is golden brown and the filling is piping hot.

To make the caramel sauce, put the sugar and a little water in a heavy-based saucepan over a high heat and swirl the pan gently until the sugar starts to colour around the edge. Do not stir at this stage or the sugar will crystallise. Swirl the pan a little more until all the sugar has dissolved and you have a dark caramel. Keep the pan on the heat and add the coconut milk, stirring as soon as it hits the caramel. Bring to the boil and stir gently until the caramel has dissolved into the coconut milk. Pour the sauce into a heatproof jug and serve with the pie.

Spiced plum and apple crumble

Crumble is a perennial favourite. It's a quick and easy pud that makes the most of whatever fruit you have available. This autumnal classic uses seasonal Bramley apples and plums.

Vegan | Serves: 4–6 | Prep: 20 minutes | Cook: 25–30 minutes

300g (10½oz) Bramley
   apples, peeled, cored
   and diced
340g (12oz) plums, halved,
   stoned and roughly
   chopped
50g (1¾oz) caster sugar
20g (¾oz) plain flour
1 tsp ground cinnamon
A pinch of grated nutmeg

Crumble topping
150g (5½oz) plain flour
70g (2½oz) porridge oats
50g (1¾oz) caster sugar
125g (4½oz) dairy-free
   baking margarine, diced
A pinch of salt
30g (1oz) demerara sugar

Preheat the oven to 190°C/180°C fan/gas 5.

Put the apples and plums in a 1.2-litre (2-pint) baking dish. In a small bowl, mix together the sugar, flour and spices; add them to the fruit and mix well.

To make the crumble topping, put the flour, oats, caster sugar, margarine and salt in a bowl and rub in the margarine until the mixture resembles fine crumbs.

Spoon the crumble mixture over the fruit and sprinkle with the demerara sugar. Bake for 25–30 minutes until the top is golden and the filling is piping hot. Spoon into serving bowls and serve with hot dairy-free custard.

COOK'S TIP

One large Bramley
apple weighs about 300g
(10½oz). Two or three
Granny Smiths would

Ginger caramel cheesecakes

Luxurious, tangy lime and ginger cheesecake with a ginger crumble base and a swirl of creamy caramel. Perfect for a winter dinner party – just pop it in the fridge to chill until you're ready to serve.

Gluten-free | Serves: 4–6 | Prep: 30 minutes | Cook: 20 minutes

Ginger crumble
125g (4½oz) gluten-free
  self-raising flour
50g (1¾oz) butter, diced
50g (1¾oz) soft dark
  brown sugar
1½ tsp ground ginger

Cheesecake
200g (7oz) condensed milk
200g (7oz) full-fat soft
  cheese
Grated zest and juice
  of 1 lime
50g (1¾oz) stem ginger
  (about 2 pieces), drained
  and chopped, plus
  syrup from the jar
100ml (3½fl oz) double
  cream

Caramel
70g (2½oz) caster sugar
55ml (2fl oz) double cream

Preheat the oven to 190°C/180°C fan/gas 5.

To make the ginger crumble, put the flour, butter, sugar and ground ginger in a bowl and rub in the butter until the mixture resembles fine crumbs. Add about ½ tbsp water so that the mixture starts to clump lightly. Tip the mixture on to a baking sheet and press into a layer. Bake for 10–15 minutes or until firm and beginning to turn golden brown at the edges. Remove from the oven and leave to cool.

To make the cheesecake, spoon the condensed milk and soft cheese into a mixing bowl, add the lime zest and juice and about 1 tbsp of the ginger syrup; whisk until the mixture thickens slightly.

In a separate bowl, whip the cream until it forms soft peaks, but do not overwhip. Add to the soft cheese mixture and whisk until thickened. Add the chopped stem ginger and stir through. Taste and add a little more ginger syrup if you like: remember that chilling tends to dull flavours.

Break up the ginger crumble using your hands or a food processor and divide between the glass serving dishes. Pipe or spoon a layer of the cream cheese mixture into each dish and place in the fridge to chill.

To make the caramel, put the sugar and 2 tsp water in a small, heavy-based pan over a high heat. Do not stir, but gently swirl the pan until the sugar starts to melt; keep swirling the pan until all the sugar has dissolved and you have a dark caramel. Pour in the cream and stir quickly until the caramel is smooth. Add a swirl of caramel over each cheesecake.

Custard tarts

With their delicate, silky filling, custard tarts are the much-loved favourites of young and old alike. Using gluten-free flour to make the pastry means that no one need miss out.

Gluten-free | Makes 12 | Prep: 25 minutes | Cook: 30–40 minutes

Gluten-free sweet pastry
250g (9oz) gluten-free
    plain flour, plus extra
    for dusting
125g (4½oz) butter, diced
3 tbsp icing sugar
A pinch of salt
2–3 tbsp cold water
A squeeze of lemon juice
Vegetable oil, for greasing

Custard
3 eggs
85g (3oz) caster sugar
1 tsp vanilla extract
200ml (7fl oz) milk
200ml (7fl oz) double
    cream
½ tsp grated nutmeg

COOK'S TIPS
This recipe uses gluten-free flour, but you could use standard plain flour.

Gluten-free pastry is quite fragile, but if it breaks as you line the tins you can patch it over with a little more pastry.

To make the pastry, put the flour, butter, icing sugar and salt into a food processor or a large bowl and mix or lightly rub in until it looks like fine crumbs. Add the water and lemon juice and stir or pulse to bring the crumbs together to make a soft dough. Lightly press into a ball, wrap in a clean, dry tea towel or beeswax wrap and chill for 10–15 minutes.

Preheat the oven to 160°C/150°C fan/gas 3 and put a baking sheet in the oven to heat up. Lightly oil a 12-hole non-stick muffin tin. Cut out 12 small circles of non-stick baking paper and line the bottoms of the tins.

Dust the work surface and the top of the pastry with flour and roll out the pastry to about 3mm (⅛ inch) thick. Cut out 12 discs using a 10cm (4 inch) cutter. Very gently press the discs into the muffin tin, using a pastry offcut dipped in flour to press into the corners (see Cook's Tips).

To make the custard, put the eggs, sugar, vanilla, milk and double cream in a bowl and whisk until smooth. Carefully pour the custard into the pastry cases, filling them to about 3mm (⅛ inch) from the top. Sprinkle the tops with a little grated nutmeg.

Place the muffin tin on the hot baking sheet and bake for 30–40 minutes, or until the custard is set but with a slight wobble.

Remove from the oven and leave to cool before removing from the tin.

Honeycomb crème brûlée

An intriguing twist on the classic crème brûlée. Making the honeycomb in advance means that you have a ready-to-go crunchy topping; it just needs a quick blast of heat until it begins to melt.

Vegetarian | Serves: 6 | Prep: 20 minutes, plus chilling | Cook: 50 minutes

400ml (14fl oz) double cream

6 egg yolks

50g (1¾oz) caster sugar

1½ tsp vanilla extract

'Honeycomb'

100g (3½oz) caster sugar

3 tbsp golden syrup

1 tsp bicarbonate of soda

COOK'S TIP

If you have a sugar thermometer, the honeycomb mixture should be 150–154°C/ 300–310°F when you add the bicarbonate of soda.

Alternatively, use the 'hard crack' test: add a drop of the mixture to a glass of cold water: it should immediately crack and set hard.

Preheat the oven to 150°C/140°C fan/gas 2.

Put the cream in a saucepan over a medium heat, bring to the boil, then reduce to a slow simmer. Meanwhile, put the egg yolks, sugar and vanilla in a bowl and whisk together until smooth.

Pour the hot cream over the egg-yolk mixture in a steady stream, whisking slowly and continuously. Strain the mixture through a sieve into a jug, then divide between six 150ml (5fl oz) ramekins.

Place the ramekins in a roasting tin and pour boiling water into the tin to come halfway up the sides of the ramekins. Bake for 30–40 minutes, or until lightly coloured on the top and almost set but with a slight wobble. Remove from the water, leave to cool, then place in the fridge to chill.

To make the honeycomb, line a small baking tin with non-stick baking paper. Put the sugar and golden syrup in a small, heavy-based pan over a low heat and stir with a wooden spoon until the sugar crystals have dissolved. Stop stirring and let the sugar bubble, swirling the pan from time to time, until it turns a rich amber colour (see Cook's Tip). Remove from the heat and immediately whisk in the bicarbonate of soda: the mixture will foam up in the pan. Stir rapidly to mix in the bicarb and then quickly but carefully pour into the lined tin and leave to set. Store in an airtight container in a cool, dry place.

To serve: preheat the grill to high or preheat the oven to 220°C/200°C fan/gas 7. Crush the honeycomb into small pieces – but do not overwork, as you don't want a powder – using a food processor (or a rolling pin). Working quickly, sprinkle the honeycomb over the baked crème brûlées, put the ramekins on a baking sheet and grill or place in the hot oven for 1–2 minutes until the honeycomb begins to melt. Serve immediately.

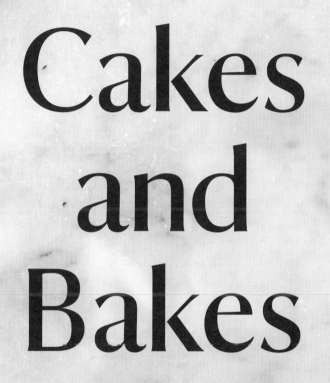

Cakes
and
Bakes

Hot cross buns

Originally these were a traditional Good Friday treat. You can't beat the homemade version, so why not start your own tradition of baking these spicy buns to start the Easter weekend?

Vegan | Makes 12 | Prep: 30 minutes, plus rising | Cook: 20–25 minutes

500g (1lb 2oz) strong white flour

2 tsp (7g sachet) fast-action dried yeast

50g (1¾oz) caster sugar

4–5 tsp ground mixed spice

½ tsp salt

200g (7oz) dried mixed fruit

About 300ml (½ pint) warm water

70g (2½oz) dairy-free baking margarine, softened

Vegetable oil, for greasing

Cross

70g (2½oz) plain flour

Glaze

3 tbsp caster sugar

3 tbsp water

Put the flour, yeast, sugar, mixed spice, salt and dried fruit in the bowl of a mixer with the dough hook fitted and mix briefly. Gradually add the warm water and mix until you have a smooth, soft dough. If you don't have an electric mixer, stir with a wooden spoon, then bring the dough together with your hands. Add the margarine and continue to knead the dough for about 4 minutes in the mixer, or turn the dough on to a lightly floured surface and knead for 8–10 minutes until it feels springy (it will be slippery at first and you will need to flour your hands, but don't worry – it will soon become kneadable).

Shape the dough into a ball. Put the dough into a floured bowl, cover with a clean tea towel and leave in a warm place for 45 minutes–1 hour until doubled in size.

Divide the dough into 12 equal pieces, roll into balls and place on a lightly oiled baking sheet. Cover and leave in a warm place for a further 45 minutes–1 hour, until the buns are risen and puffy.

Preheat the oven to 200°C/190°C fan/gas 6.

To make the cross, mix the flour with just enough cold water (about 3 tbsp) to make a stiff mixture that will hold its shape when piped. Place in a piping bag and draw crosses over the top of all the buns. Bake for 20–25 minutes until golden and risen.

To glaze, heat the sugar and water together until the sugar has dissolved. Bring to the boil, then remove from the heat and brush over the buns while they are still hot. Leave on a wire rack to cool slightly.

Rhubarb and raspberry Bakewell slice

This twist on the classic Bakewell tart makes a perfect pudding, served with generous dollops of custard. It's also great as a treat with your morning coffee or afternoon tea.

Vegetarian | Serves: 8–10 | Prep: 30 minutes | Cook: 30–40 minutes

Pastry
170g (6oz) plain flour
85g (3oz) butter, diced
30g (1oz) icing sugar
A pinch of salt
3–4 tbsp cold water

Filling
5 tbsp raspberry jam
250g (9oz) trimmed
  rhubarb, chopped
  into 2–3cm (about
  1 inch) pieces

Sponge
200g (7oz) butter, softened
200g (7oz) caster sugar
2 eggs
½ tsp almond essence
100g (3½oz) ground
  almonds
100g (3½oz) self-raising
  flour
30g (1oz) flaked almonds

To make the pastry, put the flour, butter, icing sugar and salt into a bowl or food processor and rub in or mix until it looks like fine crumbs. Add the water and stir or pulse to bring the crumbs together, then lightly knead to form a dough. Wrap in a clean, dry tea towel or beeswax wrap and chill for a good 20–30 minutes.

Preheat the oven to 180°C/170°C fan/gas 4 and line a 20cm (8 inch) square cake tin with non-stick baking paper.

On a lightly floured surface, roll out the pastry dough and use to line the base (but not the sides) of the cake tin.

For the filling, spread the jam evenly over the pastry base. Scatter the rhubarb over the jam.

To make the sponge, using an electric mixer beat the butter and sugar together until light and fluffy. Add the eggs and almond essence and beat well, then add the ground almonds and flour and mix briefly until smooth. Spoon the mixture over the filling, spreading it evenly. Sprinkle the flaked almonds over the sponge mixture.

Bake for 30–40 minutes until the sponge is golden brown and the top springs back when gently pressed. Leave to cool completely before cutting.

Lemon polenta traybake

Sunshine yellow with a zesty lemon tang, this cake makes a great gluten-free and dairy-free treat for a lunchbox or afternoon tea.

Gluten-free, Dairy-free | Makes 10 slices | Prep: 20 minutes | Cook: 20–25 minutes

150g (5½oz) dairy-free baking margarine, softened

150g (5½oz) caster sugar

3 eggs

200g (7oz) polenta

2 tsp gluten-free baking powder

Grated zest and juice of 2 lemons

Icing

100g (3½oz) icing sugar, sifted

Preheat the oven to 180°C/170°C fan/gas 4 and line a 20cm (8 inch) square cake tin with non-stick baking paper.

Using an electric mixer, beat the margarine and caster sugar together until light and fluffy. Add the eggs and mix on a low speed until incorporated, then beat well for a few seconds.

In a separate bowl, combine the polenta and baking powder and then add to the egg mixture, mixing on low speed until the mixture is light and smooth. Add the lemon zest and half the juice (reserving some for the icing) and mix well. Pour into the lined tin and smooth over the surface with a spatula. Bake for 20–25 minutes until risen and springy to the touch. Leave to cool in the tin for 5–10 minutes, then transfer to a wire rack to cool completely.

To make the icing, put the icing sugar in a small bowl and add enough of the reserved lemon juice to make a smooth icing: you may need to add a little water but take care not to make the icing too runny. Drizzle over the polenta cake and leave to set before slicing.

Banana and butterscotch cake

This moist banana bread is topped with a rich butterscotch frosting. It can be made a day or two ahead, so why not invite some friends round for coffee and a chat and a slice of this awesome cake?

Serves: 10–12 | Prep: 25 minutes | Cook: 45 minutes–1 hour

150ml (5fl oz) vegetable oil

2 eggs

150g (5½oz) soft light brown sugar

4 ripe bananas, about 400g (14oz) when peeled, mashed

½ tsp vanilla extract

200g (7oz) self-raising flour

½ tsp bicarbonate of soda

Frosting

50g (1¾oz) butter

100g (3½oz) soft light brown sugar

100ml (3½fl oz) double cream

100g (3½oz) icing sugar

Preheat the oven to 180°C/170°C fan/gas 4. Lightly grease a 900g (2lb) loaf tin, then line the base and two long sides with a piece of non-stick baking paper.

Put the oil, eggs and sugar into a bowl and whisk together until smooth. Add the bananas and vanilla and mix in, then add the flour and bicarbonate of soda, stirring gently until combined and no pockets of flour remain.

Tip the mixture into the lined tin and bake for 45 minutes–1 hour, until a skewer inserted into the centre comes out clean. Leave to cool in the tin for 10–15 minutes, then turn out on to a wire rack to cool completely.

To make the frosting, put the butter and brown sugar into a saucepan. Place over a medium heat until the butter has melted and the sugar dissolved. Remove from the heat and add the cream. This will bubble ferociously so be careful. The mixture might set and go grainy at this point, but don't worry! Return the pan to the heat and simmer gently until smooth and golden. Remove from the heat and leave to cool to room temperature. Once cooled, transfer to a food processor, add the icing sugar and mix until you have a thick, smooth frosting. Spread over the cooled cake.

Chocolate fudge cake

This vegan chocolate cake is a real crowd-pleaser, fabulously moist and simple to make. Serve it as it is with morning coffee, or decorate with fruit, nuts or chocolates for a decadent party piece.

Vegan | **Serves: 10–12** | **Prep: 30 minutes** | **Cook: 20 minutes**

370ml (12½fl oz) soya milk
1 tbsp white wine vinegar
250g (9oz) self-raising flour
50g (1¾oz) cocoa powder
250g (9oz) caster sugar
225ml (8fl oz) vegetable oil

Frosting
125g (4½oz) dairy-free
    baking margarine,
    softened
250g (9oz) icing sugar
1 tbsp vanilla extract
30g (1oz) cocoa powder

Preheat the oven to 180°C/170°C fan/gas 4. Grease two 20cm (8 inch) sandwich tins and line the bases with non-stick baking paper.

Put the soya milk in a measuring jug, add the vinegar, stir well and leave for around 10 minutes to thicken.

Sift the flour and cocoa into a large bowl, add the caster sugar and mix thoroughly. Add the thickened soya milk and oil to the dry ingredients and stir well until you have an almost smooth batter.

Divide equally between the cake tins and bake for about 20 minutes until risen and springy to the touch; a skewer inserted into the centre should come out clean. Leave to cool in the tins for about 5 minutes, then loosen the sides with a knife and turn out on to wire racks. Peel off the lining paper and then leave to cool completely.

To make the frosting, put the margarine into a mixing bowl with the icing sugar and vanilla and beat until smooth and light. Remove one-third of the frosting and set aside. Add the cocoa to the remaining frosting and mix thoroughly.

Place one of the cakes on a serving plate and spread with the vanilla frosting. Put the second cake on top and spread the top and sides of the cake with the chocolate frosting.

White chocolate, rose and raspberry blondies

The subtle floral fragrance of these irresistible blondies will transport you to a sunny afternoon in one of the National Trust's stunning rose gardens, where visitors can relax and enjoy the enchanting perfume.

Makes 9 | Prep: 30 minutes, plus cooling | Cook: 25–30 minutes

150g (5½oz) butter

100g (3½oz) white chocolate, broken into pieces

200g (7oz) caster sugar

2 eggs

1 tsp rose water

200g (7oz) plain flour

70g (2½oz) raspberries

To finish

40g (1½oz) raspberries

40g (1½oz) white chocolate, broken into small pieces

COOK'S TIPS

Keep an eye on the blondies towards the end of cooking; you want to take the tin out of the oven when the centre is still somewhat soft. They will firm up a little as they cool but will keep the squidgy texture.

For a richer, caramel-like flavour, you can swap the caster sugar for soft light brown sugar.

Preheat the oven to 180°C/170°C fan/gas 4 and line a 20cm (8 inch) square baking tin with non-stick baking paper.

Put the butter, white chocolate and sugar in a large saucepan over a low heat until the chocolate has melted and the sugar has dissolved, stirring regularly. Leave to cool for 5–10 minutes.

Once the chocolate mixture has cooled slightly, beat in the eggs one by one, followed by the rose water, and mix thoroughly. Sift the flour over the mixture and fold through until combined. Add the raspberries and fold until rippled through the mixture.

Pour the mixture into the lined tin and top with the remaining raspberries and white chocolate. Use a spoon to gently swirl them through the mixture. Bake for 20–25 minutes until the top is golden and the cake is just set, with a slight wobble.

Remove from the oven and leave to cool in the tin before cutting into pieces.

Marbled loaf cake

This impressive cake is easy to make, using the all-in-one sponge method. There's no need to be too precise when dividing the basic mixture in half, as the chocolate and vanilla mixes swirl together as they bake.

Serves: 10–12 | Prep: 20 minutes | Cook: 45–50 minutes

170g (6oz) butter, softened, plus extra for greasing

170g (6oz) caster sugar

3 eggs

170g (6oz) self-raising flour

1 tsp baking powder

2 tbsp cocoa powder

3 tbsp water

2 tsp vanilla extract

Preheat the oven to 180°C/170°C fan/gas 4. Lightly butter a 900g (2lb) loaf tin and line the base and two long sides with a piece of non-stick baking paper.

Mix the butter, sugar and eggs in a bowl (use an electric mixer if you have one). Sift the flour and baking powder into the bowl and use a spoon to gently combine, then beat thoroughly until the mixture is light and fluffy (see Cook's Tips). Put half the mixture into another bowl.

Mix the cocoa and water together in a cup until smooth, then add to half of the cake mixture and mix well. Add the vanilla to the remaining mixture and mix well. Place spoonfuls of each mixture randomly in the tin until it is all used up. Gently tap and shake the tin to level the mixture and then swirl a skewer through it once or twice. Bake for 45–50 minutes until a skewer inserted into the centre comes out clean.

Leave to cool in the tin for 10 minutes, and then turn out onto a wire rack to cool completely.

COOK'S TIPS

Make sure that you beat the mixture for at least 3 minutes to reach full volume.

This freezes well as a whole cake, but not in slices as they dry out more quickly.

Lavender shortbread

Combining the calming aroma of lavender with the crisp yet crumbly texture of buttery shortbread, this beautiful bake is simply irresistible.

Makes 10–12 | Prep: 30 minutes | Cook: 15–20 minutes

Shortbread
300g (10½oz) plain flour
200g (7oz) butter, slightly
    softened
100g (3½oz) caster sugar
1–2 tsp dried lavender
    flowers

Topping
50g (1¾oz) icing sugar
½ tsp dried lavender
    flowers

Preheat the oven to 160°C/150°C fan/gas 3 and line a loose-bottomed, shallow 23cm (9 inch) tart tin with non-stick baking paper.

Put the shortbread ingredients into the bowl of a mixer or food processor and mix on a low speed until just coming together.

Tip out on to a work surface and bring together to form a dough. Put the dough into the lined tart tin and spread out evenly, pressing firmly but gently.

Bake for 15–20 minutes until golden and set. While still warm, use a long, thin knife to lightly mark out 10–12 portions. Carefully remove from the tin (the shortbread will still be soft) and leave on a wire rack to cool completely.

To make the topping, sift the icing sugar into a small bowl and add a teaspoon or so of water – just enough water to make a thick but pourable icing. Drizzle the icing over the shortbread. Sprinkle over the lavender flowers, pressing down slightly so that they stick to the icing.

Use a long, thin, sharp knife to cut out the marked portions.

COOK'S TIP
Instead of lavender, you could flavour the shortbread with 1 tsp fresh thyme leaves and the grated zest of 1 lemon; use the lemon juice to make the icing.

Orange and lemon cake

This lovely variation on a Victoria sponge has a delicate orange flavour which is echoed in the orange syrup that's brushed over. The simple buttercream filling is topped with a layer of zingy lemon curd.

Serves: 8 | Prep: 30 minutes | Cook: 20–25 minutes

170g (6oz) butter, softened
170g (6oz) caster sugar
Grated zest of 1 orange
3 eggs, beaten
170g (6oz) self-raising flour
½ tsp baking powder

Orange syrup
Grated zest and juice
   of 1 orange
55g (2oz) caster sugar

Filling
70g (2½oz) butter, softened
150g (5½oz) icing sugar
4 tbsp lemon curd

To decorate (optional)
1 orange, rind peeled in
   thin strips (avoiding
   the pith)
55g (2oz) caster sugar
6 tbsp water

Preheat the oven to 190°C/180°C fan/gas 5. Grease two 20cm (8 inch) sandwich tins and line the bases with non-stick baking paper.

Put the butter and sugar in a bowl and beat together until light and fluffy (use an electric mixer if you have one). Add the orange zest.

Gradually beat in the eggs, little by little, beating well after each addition and adding a spoonful of the flour with each addition to stabilise the mixture.

Sift the remaining flour and the baking powder over the cake mixture and gently fold in until smooth. If needed, add a little orange juice so the mixture has a dropping consistency. Divide equally between the tins and gently level the surface. Bake for 20–25 minutes until well risen and the tops spring back when gently pressed with a fingertip.

Leave to cool in the tins for 5 minutes, then loosen the sides and turn out, peeling off the lining paper. Leave on a wire rack to cool completely.

To make the orange syrup, mix the orange zest and juice with the caster sugar and stir until dissolved.

To make the filling, beat the softened butter and icing sugar together until light and fluffy.

To decorate (if you like), put the orange rind, sugar and water in a small saucepan, bring to a simmer and cook for 5–7 minutes. Drain. Place one of the cakes on a serving plate or board (if the top is domed, cut off a slice to make it flat). Brush half of the orange syrup over the sponge. Spread the filling over the sponge, followed by the lemon curd. Put the second cake on top, brush over the remaining orange syrup, and decorate with the orange rind, if desired.

Coconut and raisin flapjacks

These chewy, oaty bars are ideal as an energy-boosting snack or breakfast on the go. The coconut and juicy raisins keep them extra moist – you can substitute cherries, sultanas or apricots.

Vegan | Makes 12 | Prep: 20 minutes, plus cooling | Cook: 25–30 minutes

85g (3oz) desiccated
  coconut
85ml (3fl oz) boiling water
85g (3oz) raisins
150g (5½oz) dairy-free
  baking margarine
85g (3oz) caster sugar
125g (4½oz) golden syrup
300g (10½oz) porridge oats

Preheat the oven to 180°C/170°C fan/gas 4. Grease a 20cm (8 inch) square cake tin and line with non-stick baking paper.

Put the coconut in a bowl and add the boiling water. Stir well and leave to stand for a few minutes. Add the raisins and stir again. Put to one side while you prepare the rest of the ingredients.

Put the margarine, sugar and syrup in a large saucepan over a low–medium heat, stirring from time to time, until the sugar has dissolved (see Cook's Tips). Add the soaked coconut and raisins and mix well, then remove from the heat.

Add the oats and stir well until all the ingredients are evenly mixed. Tip into the lined tin and gently press the surface level. Bake for 20–25 minutes until lightly coloured and just set. Remove from the oven and leave to cool in the tin for about 30 minutes, then mark into bars or squares. Leave in the tin to cool completely before cutting into pieces. You can store them in an airtight container for up to a week.

COOK'S TIPS

Some people who must avoid gluten can tolerate oats – just make sure that the pack carries the gluten-free symbol as not all oats are packaged in factories that are gluten-free.

Don't boil the syrup mixture: boiling will make the flapjack too crispy.

For colourful flapjacks, you can replace the raisins with dried cherries or chopped dried apricots. Alternatively, use halved glacé cherries.

Damson traybake

This simple mixture magically creates a crisp, buttery biscuit base with a dense cake topping. Damsons have an intense, sharp flavour which contrasts with the fudgy sweetness of this bake.

Serves: 10–12 | Prep: 15 minutes | Cook: about 35–40 minutes

300g (10½oz) soft light
  brown sugar
300g (10½oz) self-raising
  flour
150g (5½oz) butter, diced
250ml (9fl oz) soured
  cream
2 eggs
300g (10½oz) damsons,
  halved and stoned

Preheat the oven to 180°C/170°C fan/gas 4. Line a 20cm (8 inch) square cake tin with non-stick baking paper.

Mix the sugar and flour together and then rub in the butter until you have a sandy texture.

Spread half the mixture into the bottom of the lined cake tin, gently pressing down and making it as even as possible.

Whisk together the soured cream and eggs. Add to the remaining flour mixture and stir together until just combined and only a few lumps remain. Pour the mixture over the base and tilt the tin to spread evenly. Scatter the damsons over the surface. Bake for 35–40 minutes until golden and springy to the touch.

Leave to cool in the tin before cutting into slices.

COOK'S TIPS

If you can't get damsons, try greengages or other plums.

At other times of the year you might like to try this with chopped rhubarb, halved gooseberries, or mixed summer berries – ideally including some blackcurrants. You should only need about 200g (7oz) as these fruits don't have stones.

Chocolate chip cookies

With their gooey melting middles, these cookies will be popular at any time of day – from morning coffee to midnight feast!

Vegan | Makes 12 | Prep: 15 minutes | Cook: 10–12 minutes

250g (9oz) dairy-free
   baking margarine,
   softened
100g (3½oz) caster sugar
60g (2¼oz) soft dark
   brown sugar
60g (2¼oz) golden syrup
1½ tsp vanilla extract
370g (13oz) self-raising
   flour
50g (1¾oz) cocoa powder
100g (3½oz) vegan
   chocolate chips

Preheat the oven to 180°C/170°C fan/gas 4. Line a baking sheet with non-stick baking paper.

Beat the margarine and both sugars together with an electric whisk, if you have one, until light and fluffy. Add the golden syrup and vanilla and beat again.

Add the flour and cocoa and mix gently until incorporated. Add the chocolate chips and mix until combined.

Use an ice-cream scoop to measure out balls of the mixture – approximately 70g (2½oz) each – on to the lined baking sheet, spacing them well apart, and then pat gently to flatten.

Bake for about 10–12 minutes until cracks appear: the cookies will be very soft, but will firm up as they cool. Remove from the oven and leave to cool on the baking sheet for about 5 minutes before transferring them to a wire rack to cool completely.

COOK'S TIP

Don't overcook these: the cookies should be soft when you remove them from the oven. They will firm up as they cool but should remain moist and chewy in the centre.

Pumpkin pie scones

Moist and mildly spicy, these generously sized scones will be a welcome treat for an autumn afternoon tea. Serve while still warm from the oven, with butter.

Makes 10 | Prep: 25 minutes | Cook: 18–20 minutes

Vegetable oil, for greasing

500g (1lb 2oz) self-raising flour, plus extra for dusting

2 tsp baking powder

125g (4½oz) soft light brown sugar

1 tsp ground cinnamon

¼ tsp grated nutmeg

100g (3½oz) butter, diced

125g (4½oz) grated fresh pumpkin or canned pumpkin purée

1 tsp vanilla extract

3 tbsp milk

1 egg, beaten

200g (7oz) condensed milk

Preheat the oven to 200°C/190°C fan/gas 6 and lightly oil a baking sheet. Put the flour, baking powder, sugar, spices and butter into a food processor and blitz until the mixture resembles fine crumbs. Alternatively, put the ingredients into a large mixing bowl and rub in the butter with your fingertips.

Add the grated pumpkin and vanilla and mix briefly.

Using a fork, mix the milk and egg together in a jug. Take out 1 tbsp and set aside for glazing the tops. Mix in the condensed milk. Make a hollow in the pumpkin mixture and gradually pour in the liquid, adding enough to form a soft but not sticky dough (you may not need to use all of the liquid).

Turn out the dough on to a lightly floured surface and roll out to 3–4cm (1¼–1½ inches) thick. Using a 7cm (2¾ inch) round cutter, stamp out the scones and transfer to the baking sheet (see Cook's Tip). Gently re-roll the trimmings to make more scones. Brush the tops with the reserved egg mixture, then bake for 18–20 minutes until risen and springy to the touch: a small sharp knife inserted into the side should come out clean. Leave on a wire rack to cool slightly before serving.

COOK'S TIP

Dip the cutter in flour before cutting out each scone.

Spiced toffee apple cake

Why celebrate Apple Day just once a year? Many National Trust properties have glorious orchards growing a variety of heritage apples; some ripen early, while others are ready later in the season.

Gluten-free | Serves: 12 | Prep: 30 minutes | Cook: about 1 hour

170g (6oz) pitted dates

150ml (5fl oz) milk

2 small dessert apples

Juice of ½ lemon

200g (7oz) butter, softened

225g (8oz) gluten-free
self-raising flour

¾ tsp gluten-free baking
powder

170g (6oz) soft light
brown sugar

4 eggs

2 tsp ground mixed spice

1 tsp vanilla extract

Toffee sauce

50g (1¾oz) soft light
brown sugar

50g (1¾oz) butter

2 tbsp double cream

Preheat the oven to 180°C/170°C fan/gas 4. Grease a 23cm (9 inch) springform tin and line the base with non-stick baking paper.

Put the dates and milk in a saucepan over a medium heat and bring to the boil, then immediately reduce to a simmer and cook for 2–3 minutes until the dates are soft. Remove from the heat and purée until smooth using a stick blender or a liquidiser (see Cook's Tips). Set aside and leave until completely cold.

Peel, core and finely slice the apples. Drop the slices into a bowl with the lemon juice and toss to coat.

Put the butter, flour, baking powder, sugar, eggs, mixed spice and vanilla into a bowl. Add the date purée and use an electric mixer to beat until light and fluffy. Pour the mixture into the tin and arrange the apple slices on top in overlapping rings. Bake for 50 minutes–1 hour until a skewer inserted into the centre comes out clean. Remove from the oven and leave to cool.

To make the toffee sauce, put the sugar, butter and cream in a saucepan over a medium heat, stirring occasionally until the sugar has dissolved. Increase the heat and simmer for 1–2 minutes until the sauce begins to thicken, then remove from the heat: it will thicken further as it cools.

To serve, pour the sauce over the cake and, if you like, serve with cream or ice cream.

COOK'S TIPS

Take care when blending the dates as there may be the odd stone.

Don't open the oven door for at least the first 40 minutes of cooking.

Lemon and hazelnut upside down cake

A retro favourite given a makeover! Eggless and dairy-free, with hazelnuts to keep the cake moist and wafer-thin slices of lemon revealed when you turn it upside down.

Vegan | Serves: 10–12 | **Prep: 30 minutes** | **Cook: 35 minutes**

200g (7oz) blanched hazelnuts

2 lemons: grated zest and juice of 1, the other thinly sliced and pips discarded

400g (14oz) self-raising flour

1 tsp baking powder

¾ tsp bicarbonate of soda

A pinch of salt

150g (5½oz) caster sugar

120ml (4fl oz) vegetable oil

225ml (8fl oz) soya milk

1 tbsp vanilla extract

50g (1¾oz) dairy-free baking margarine, melted

3 tbsp golden syrup

3 tsp boiling water

Preheat the oven to 220°C/200°C fan/gas 7.

Put the hazelnuts on a baking sheet and toast them in the oven for 3–4 minutes until lightly golden. Remove from the oven and leave to cool. Blitz the nuts in a food processor until finely ground.

Turn the oven down to 190°C/180°C fan/gas 5. Line a 23cm (9 inch) springform tin with non-stick baking paper. Arrange the lemon slices in the bottom.

Put the flour, baking powder, bicarbonate of soda, salt, caster sugar and blitzed hazelnuts in a bowl and mix well.

Put the lemon zest and juice, vegetable oil, soya milk and vanilla in a separate large bowl and whisk until combined.

Tip the dry ingredients into the wet and fold through until smooth. Add the melted margarine and stir through again.

Tip the batter into the tin, taking care not to disturb the lemon slices, then bake for about 30 minutes until risen and springy to the touch; a skewer inserted into the centre should come out clean.

Leave to cool in the tin for a few minutes. Run a spatula around the side of the tin to loosen the cake. Place a serving plate on top of the tin, turn the cake over and remove the tin. Peel off the lining paper.

Mix the golden syrup with the boiling water and then brush over the cake. Leave to cool completely before slicing.

COOK'S TIP

This cake isn't suitable for freezing as it dries out significantly.

Tea-soaked fruit cake

This no-nonsense fruit cake is good at any time of year. It's easy to make, not too sweet, keeps well and is equally at home on the tea table, as part of a packed lunch or in a picnic hamper.

Dairy-free | Serves: 10–12 | Prep: 10 minutes, plus soaking | Cook: 1 hour 30 minutes

3 teabags

120ml (4fl oz) boiling water

250g (9oz) mixed dried
  fruit

270g (9½oz) self-raising
  flour

A good pinch of salt

170g (6oz) dairy-free
  baking margarine, diced

125g (4½oz) caster sugar

2 tsp ground mixed spice

3 eggs, beaten

Put the teabags in a bowl, add the boiling water and stir to make a very strong tea. Add the dried fruit, stir well and leave to soak until the liquid is cold. You can leave the fruit to soak overnight.

Remove the teabags, squeezing out the tea, give the fruit a stir and then put to one side.

Preheat the oven to 180°C/170°C fan/gas 4. Lightly grease a 900g (2lb) loaf tin and line the base and two long sides with a piece of non-stick baking paper.

Put the flour and salt in a large bowl, add the margarine and rub in until the mixture resembles fine crumbs (see Cook's Tip). Add the sugar and mixed spice and stir well.

Add the eggs and the soaked fruit, along with any remaining liquid, and stir until evenly combined. Spoon the mixture into the lined tin. Bake for 1¼–1½ hours or until the cake is risen, golden brown and a skewer inserted into the centre comes out clean.

Leave to cool in the tin for about 10 minutes, then turn out on to a wire rack and leave to cool completely before slicing.

COOK'S TIP

Save time by using a food processor to rub in the margarine – but tip the mixture into a large bowl to add the sugar, spice, eggs and soaked fruit.

Gingerbread biscuits

Make gingerbread people or animals for a children's party, stars for teenagers and hearts for Valentine's Day. You can get as creative as you like with icing and decorating the biscuits.

Makes 10–20 biscuits | Prep: 30 minutes, plus chilling | Cook: 10 minutes

350g (12½oz) plain flour,
   plus extra for dusting
1 tsp bicarbonate of soda
A pinch of salt
2 tsp ground ginger
1 tsp ground cinnamon
125g (4½oz) butter, diced
150g (5½oz) soft light
   brown sugar
1 egg
4 tbsp golden syrup

Icing
200g (7oz) icing sugar
2–3 tsp just-boiled water

COOK'S TIPS

Oil your measuring spoon before pouring in the golden syrup: it will then slide off easily.

   You don't have to bake all the dough at once: it can be wrapped and stored in the fridge for up to a week, ready to bake a fresh batch of biscuits.

Line one or two large baking sheets with non-stick baking paper.

Sift the flour, bicarbonate of soda, salt and spices into a bowl or food processor. Add the butter and mix or rub in until it resembles fine crumbs. Stir in the light brown sugar.

Lightly beat the egg and syrup together, add to the dry ingredients and mix until you have a dough. Wrap in a clean, dry tea towel or beeswax wrap and chill in the fridge for at least 20 minutes.

Preheat the oven to 180°C/170°C fan/gas 4.

On a lightly floured surface, roll out the dough to about 5mm (¼ inch) thick, cut out the biscuits and place on a lined baking sheet, spacing them well apart. Re-roll the trimmings to make more biscuits.

Bake the biscuits for 8–10 minutes until they are just beginning to brown at the edges. Leave on the baking sheet for about 10 minutes until they begin to firm up. Using a palette knife, carefully transfer them to a wire rack to cool completely.

To make the icing, mix the icing sugar with the just-boiled water until you have a thick, smooth icing. Pipe or drizzle the icing over the biscuits.

White chocolate brownies

Everyone loves a squidgy brownie: these are rich, gluten-free and super easy to make.
The hardest part will be waiting for them to cool before you eat them.

Gluten-free | Makes 12 slices | Prep: 15 minutes | Cook: 20 minutes

170g (6oz) dairy-free
    baking margarine
280g (10oz) caster sugar
60g (2¼oz) cocoa powder
3 eggs, beaten
115g (4oz) gluten-free
    self-raising flour
100g (3½oz) white
    chocolate, chopped
    into small pieces

Preheat the oven to 180°C/170°C fan/gas 4. Grease a 20cm (8 inch) square cake tin and line with non-stick baking paper.

Heat the margarine in a saucepan over a low heat until melted. Remove from the heat, add the sugar and cocoa and mix thoroughly. Add the beaten eggs and beat until smooth. Add the flour and beat until smooth. Pour into the lined tin.

Sprinkle the white chocolate over the brownie mixture. Bake for about 20 minutes until risen slightly and just set, with a slight wobble.

Leave in the tin to cool completely before cutting into pieces.

COOK'S TIP

Keep an eye on the brownies towards the end of cooking: you want to take them out of the oven when the centre is still slightly soft. They will firm up a little as they cool but will keep that gooey brownie texture.

Chocolate and marmalade slice

Light gluten-free sponge topped with tangy orange and a layer of chocolate, this is a real treat for elevenses or teatime – and so much nicer than anything you get from a packet!

Gluten-free | **Makes 10 slices** | **Prep: 20 minutes** | **Cook: 20–25 minutes**

170g (6oz) salted butter or baking margarine, softened

200g (7oz) gluten-free self-raising flour

170g (6oz) caster sugar

3 eggs

Topping

250g (9oz) orange marmalade

100ml (3½fl oz) double cream

150g (5½oz) dark chocolate, broken into small pieces

Preheat the oven to 190°C/180°C fan/gas 5. Grease a 20cm (8 inch) square cake tin and line with non-stick baking paper.

Put the butter in a large bowl, sift over the flour, then add the sugar and eggs. Using an electric mixer, whisk together until light and fluffy (see Cook's Tips). Tip the mixture into the lined tin and smooth over the surface with a spatula.

Bake for 20–25 minutes until risen and firm to the touch; a skewer inserted into the centre should come out clean. Remove from the oven and leave to cool in the tin.

Tip the marmalade into a bowl and whisk briefly with a fork until smooth, then pour it over the top of the sponge. Place in the fridge to chill and set.

Heat the cream in a small saucepan and add the chocolate. Leave for a minute or two, then stir gently until completely melted and smooth. Leave to cool slightly, then pour over the cake, gently spreading with a palette knife. Leave to cool and set completely. To remove from the tin, use the edges of the baking paper to lift the cake onto a board before slicing.

COOK'S TIPS

Make sure that you beat the mixture for at least 3 minutes to reach full volume.

Swap the dark chocolate for milk chocolate if you prefer.

Cranberry and orange cake

A real showstopper, this cake is studded with cranberries, filled with almond buttercream and topped with orange glacé icing.

Vegan | Serves: 10–12 | Prep: 1 hour | Cook: 40 minutes

185g (6½oz) dairy-free baking margarine

300ml (½ pint) soya milk

1 tbsp white wine vinegar

300g (10½oz) self-raising flour

1 tsp baking powder

1 tsp ground ginger

1 tsp ground cinnamon

225g (8oz) caster sugar

Grated zest and juice of 1 orange

70g (2½oz) dried cranberries

50g (1¾oz) icing sugar

Frosting

125g (4½oz) dairy-free baking margarine, softened

250g (9oz) icing sugar

½ tsp almond essence

Toppings

200g (7oz) icing sugar

1 orange, juice

60g (2¼oz) caster sugar

60g (2¼oz) dried cranberries

Orange rind, peeled, to decorate (optional)

Preheat the oven to 180°C/170°C fan/gas 4. Grease three 20cm (8 inch) sandwich tins and line the bases with non-stick baking paper.

Melt the margarine over a low heat, then put to one side. Put the soya milk in a jug, add the vinegar, stir well and leave to thicken. Sift the flour, baking powder and spices into a large bowl, then stir in the caster sugar and orange zest. Make a well in the centre and pour in the melted margarine, the curdled soya milk and the cranberries and stir until well mixed. Divide the mixture between the three tins and bake for 20–30 minutes or until risen and springy to the touch; a skewer inserted into the centre should come out clean.

Mix the icing sugar with half of the orange juice until dissolved. Prick the warm cakes all over with a skewer and pour a third of the orange juice mixture over each one. Leave to cool.

To make the frosting, using an electric mixer, beat the margarine, icing sugar and almond essence together on low speed until smooth. Increase the speed and beat until light and fluffy, adding a drop of water if the mixture seems too thick: it should have the consistency of whipped double cream. Remove the cakes from the tins. Place one cake on a plate and spread with a third of the frosting. Put a second cake on top and spread with another third. Add the third cake and spread the remaining frosting over the whole lot (this should be a thin layer).

For the toppings, sift the icing sugar into a bowl and add the orange juice, a little at a time, until you have a thick, smooth icing. Pour over the top of the cake and leave to set. Put the caster sugar in a small saucepan, add 4 tbsp water and bring to the boil. Add the cranberries and simmer gently for about 10 minutes, until the syrup is thick and reduced and the cranberries are soft. Leave to cool. Prepare the orange rind as on page 139. Sprinkle the cranberries and orange rind over the cake to finish.

Index

Vegan and vegetarian recipes
in **bold**

A

almonds
   peach frangipane tart **111**
   potato, leek and almond
      salad with soured cream
      dressing **35**
   rhubarb and raspberry
      Bakewell slice **128**
apples
   apple and pear pie with
      caramel sauce **117**
   pickled red cabbage
      salad with smoked
      mackerel **39**
   pork, apple and sage pies 59
   roasted vegetable soup with
      apple slices **28**
   spiced plum and apple
      crumble **119**
   spiced toffee apple cake **146**
apricots: Moroccan-style chicken
   stew 81
aquafaba: beetroot, carrot and
   spring onion fritters **50**
asparagus: spring vegetable
   pasta alfredo **75**
aubergines
   ratatouille with pistou **82**
   roasted aubergine with
      chickpea salad and chilli
      caramelised nuts **40**

B

bacon
   Brussels sprout, bacon and
      chestnut salad 43
   cheese, bacon and chive
      scones 49
   game and celeriac stew 97
   hunter's chicken 80
banana and butterscotch
   cake **131**
barley: wild mushroom and
   barley soup **22**
beans
   chilli non carne **95**
   lentil and green bean salad
      with ginger dressing **34**
   spring vegetable pasta
      alfredo **75**
beef, ale and horseradish
   cobbler 102
beetroot
   beetroot, carrot and spring
      onion fritters **50**
   roasted beetroot, kale
      and Brie quiche **65**
   roasted beetroot with
      walnuts and Stilton **45**
berries: summer berry tart **114**
biscuits
   chocolate chip cookies **142**
   gingerbread biscuits **151**
   lavender shortbread **137**
blueberry and lemon mousse
   pot **107**

C

cabbage
   pickled red cabbage
      salad with smoked
      mackerel **39**
   red cabbage salad 101
   Thai-style green curry
      soup **16**
carrots
   beetroot, carrot and spring
      onion fritters **50**
   chicken, leek and tarragon
      pie 85
   game and celeriac stew 97

bread
   basil and goat's cheese
      twists **55**
   bread pudding **110**
   croque monsieur 66
   flatbreads 101
   Tuscan-style tomato
      soup **19**
broad beans: spring vegetable
   pasta alfredo **75**
broccoli
   lentil and green bean salad
      with ginger dressing **34**
   pea, broccoli and rocket
      tart **52**
   spring vegetable pasta
      alfredo **75**
Brussels sprout, bacon and
   chestnut salad 43

harissa carrot salad **36**
lamb hotpot **76**
lentil and green bean salad
   with ginger dressing **34**
Moroccan-style chicken
   stew **81**
pickled red cabbage
   salad with smoked
   mackerel **39**
roasted red pepper soup **21**
roasted vegetable soup
   with apple slices **28**
spicy carrot and coconut
   soup **25**
summer veg filo tarts **56**
cashews: harissa carrot salad **36**
cauliflower
   cauliflower, turmeric and
      coconut soup **27**
   coronation cauliflower
      and couscous salad **42**
   roasted cauliflower mac
      and cheese **88**
   spiced cauliflower and potato
      parcels **61**
   sweet potato and cauliflower
      curry pies **78**
celeriac: game and celeriac
   stew **97**
celery
   beef, ale and horseradish
      cobbler **102**
   lamb hotpot **76**
   oxtail soup **26**
cheese
   basil and goat's cheese
      twists **55**
   cheese, bacon and chive
      scones **49**
   courgette, fennel, olive
      and feta frittata **53**
   croque monsieur **66**
   goat's cheese and tabbouleh
      salad **33**
   ham, leek and Cheddar
      crumble **98**
   nut roast **96**

onion soup **15**
pea, broccoli and rocket tart **52**
pear, walnut and Stilton
   quiches **69**
roasted beetroot, kale and
   Brie quiche **65**
roasted beetroot with
   walnuts and Stilton **45**
roasted cauliflower mac
   and cheese **88**
spring vegetable pasta
   alfredo **75**
squash, feta and sage filo
   bake **62**
cheesecakes
   baked rhubarb and ginger
      cheesecake **108**
   ginger caramel cheesecakes **120**
chestnuts: Brussels sprout, bacon
   and chestnut salad **43**
chicken
   chicken, leek and tarragon
      pie **85**
   chicken souvlaki with
      tzatziki **84**
   hunter's chicken **80**
   Moroccan-style chicken
      stew **81**
chickpeas
   harissa carrot salad **36**
   Moroccan-style chicken
      stew **81**
   mushroom and cranberry
      rolls **70**
   roasted aubergine with
      chickpea salad and chilli
      caramelised nuts **40**
   spiced cauliflower and potato
      parcels **61**
   sweet potato and cauliflower
      curry pies **78**
chilli non carne **95**
chocolate
   chocolate and marmalade slice
      153
   chocolate chip cookies **142**
   chocolate fudge cake **133**

white chocolate brownies **152**
white chocolate, rose and
   raspberry blondies **134**
cobbler, beef, ale and horseradish
   102
coconut and raisin flapjacks **140**
coconut milk
   cauliflower, turmeric and
      coconut soup **27**
   spicy carrot and coconut
      soup **25**
   sweet potato and cauliflower
      curry pies **78**
   Thai-style green curry soup **16**
courgettes
   courgette, fennel, olive
      and feta frittata **53**
   courgette, pea and basil soup
      20
   ratatouille with pistou **82**
   summer veg filo tarts **56**
couscous: coronation cauliflower
   and couscous salad **42**
cranberries
   Brussels sprout, bacon
      and chestnut salad **43**
   cranberry and orange
      cake **154**
   mushroom and cranberry
      rolls **70**
   nut roast **96**
cream cheese
   baked rhubarb and ginger
      cheesecake **108**
   ginger caramel cheesecakes
      120
   roasted beetroot with
      walnuts and Stilton **45**
crème brûlée, honeycomb **123**
croque monsieur **66**
crumble
   spiced plum and apple
      crumble **119**
   ham, leek and Cheddar
      crumble **98**
custard tarts **122**

D

damson traybake 141
dates: spiced toffee apple
  cake 146

E

eggs
  courgette, fennel, olive
    and feta frittata 53
  custard tarts 122
  pea and mint Scotch eggs 48
  pea, broccoli and rocket
    tart 52
  pear, walnut and Stilton
    quiches 69
  roasted beetroot, kale
    and Brie quiche 65
  smoked salmon and
    watercress quiche 60

F

fennel
  courgette, fennel, olive
    and feta frittata 53
  pickled red cabbage
    salad with smoked
    mackerel 39
  ratatouille with pistou 82
fish
  pickled red cabbage
    salad with smoked
    mackerel 39
  smoked salmon and
    watercress quiche 60
flapjacks, coconut and raisin 140
fruit cake, tea-soaked 149

G

game and celeriac stew 97
ginger
  baked rhubarb and ginger
    cheesecake 108
  coronation cauliflower
    and couscous salad 42
  ginger caramel cheesecakes
    120
  gingerbread biscuits 151

lentil and green bean salad
  with ginger dressing 34
spicy carrot and coconut
  soup 25
gingerbread biscuits 151
green beans: lentil and green
  bean salad with ginger
  dressing 34

H

ham
  croque monsieur 66
  ham, leek and Cheddar
    crumble 98
hazelnuts: lemon and hazelnut
  upside down cake 148
honeycomb crème brûlée 123
horseradish: beef, ale and
  horseradish cobbler 102
hot cross buns 127

K

kale
  honey-roast squash, pearl
    barley and kale 90–1
  roasted beetroot, kale
    and Brie quiche 65

L

lamb
  lamb hotpot 76
  slow-roast spiced shoulder
    of lamb 101
lavender
  lavender and honey
    panna cotta 113
  lavender shortbread 137
leeks
  chicken, leek and tarragon
    pie 85
  courgette, pea and basil
    soup 20
  ham, leek and Cheddar
    crumble 98
  potato, leek and almond
    salad with soured cream
    dressing 35

Thai-style green curry
  soup 16
lemons
  blueberry and lemon mousse
    pot 107
  goat's cheese and tabbouleh
    salad 33
  lemon and hazelnut upside
    down cake 148
  lemon polenta traybake 130
  orange and lemon cake 139
lentils
  chilli non carne 95
  lentil and green bean
    salad with ginger
    dressing 34

M

mackerel: pickled red
  cabbage salad with
  smoked mackerel 39
mangetout
  spring vegetable pasta
    alfredo 75
  Thai-style green curry
    soup 16
marbled loaf cake 136
mayonnaise, vegan 50
mushrooms
  beef, ale and horseradish
    cobbler 102
  chilli non carne 95
  ham, leek and Cheddar
    crumble 98
  hunter's chicken 80
  mushroom and cranberry
    rolls 70
  mushroom suet puddings
    92–3
  nut roast 96
  pork stroganoff 77
  wild mushroom and barley
    soup 22

N

noodles: Thai-style green
  curry soup 16

nuts
 harissa carrot salad **36**
 lemon and hazelnut upside
  down cake **148**
 nut roast **96**
 pear, walnut and Stilton
  quiches **69**
 potato, leek and almond
  salad with soured cream
  dressing **35**
 rhubarb and raspberry
  Bakewell slice **128**
 roasted aubergine with
  chickpea salad and chilli
  caramelised nuts **40**
 roasted beetroot with walnuts
  and Stilton **45**

O

oats: coconut and raisin
 flapjacks **140**
olives: courgette, fennel,
 olive and feta frittata **53**
onions
 hunter's chicken **80**
 Moroccan-style chicken
  stew **81**
 mushroom and cranberry
  rolls **70**
 mushroom suet puddings
  92–3
 nut roast **96**
 onion soup **15**
 oxtail soup **26**
 pork stroganoff **77**
 ratatouille with pistou **82**
 roasted red pepper soup **21**
 roasted vegetable soup with
  apple slices **28**
 summer veg filo tarts **56**
oranges
 Brussels sprout, bacon
  and chestnut salad **43**
 cranberry and orange
  cake **154**
 harissa carrot salad **36**
 orange and lemon cake **139**

pickled red cabbage
 salad with smoked
 mackerel **39**
poached pears **116**
roasted beetroot, kale
 and Brie **65**
oxtail soup **26**

P

panna cotta, lavender and
 honey **113**
parsnips: roasted vegetable
 soup with apple slices **28**
pasta
 roasted cauliflower mac
  and cheese **88**
 sausage and fennel-seed
  pasta **99**
 spring vegetable pasta
  alfredo **75**
peach frangipane tart **111**
pearl barley
 goat's cheese and tabbouleh
  salad **33**
 honey-roast squash, pearl
  barley and kale **90–1**
pears
 pear, walnut and Stilton
  quiches **69**
 poached pears **116**
peas
 courgette, pea and basil
  soup **20**
 pea and mint Scotch
  eggs **48**
 pea, broccoli and rocket
  tart **52**
 summer veg filo tarts **56**
peppers
 chilli non carne **95**
 coronation cauliflower
  and couscous salad **42**
 ratatouille with pistou **82**
 roasted red pepper soup **21**
 summer veg filo tarts **56**
 Tuscan-style tomato
  soup **19**

pies
 apple and pear pie with
  caramel sauce **117**
 chicken, leek and tarragon
  pie **85**
 pork, apple and sage pies **59**
 sweet potato and cauliflower
  curry pies **78**
plums
 damson traybake **141**
 spiced plum and apple
  crumble **119**
polenta
 lemon polenta traybake **130**
 mushroom and cranberry
  rolls **70**
 sticky sausages and polenta
  chips **87**
pomegranate: goat's cheese and
 tabbouleh salad **33**
pork
 pork, apple and sage
  pies **59**
 pork stroganoff **77**
potatoes
 courgette, fennel, olive
  and feta frittata **53**
 ham, leek and Cheddar
  crumble **98**
 lamb hotpot **76**
 potato, leek and almond
  salad with soured cream
  dressing **35**
 spiced cauliflower and potato
  parcels **61**
 wild garlic soup **14**
prunes: game and celeriac
 stew **97**
pumpkin pie scones **145**

Q

quiche
 pear, walnut and Stilton **69**
 roasted beetroot, kale and
  Brie **65**
 smoked salmon and
  watercress **60**

R

raspberries
  rhubarb and raspberry
    Bakewell slice **128**
  summer berry tart **114**
  white chocolate, rose and
    raspberry blondies **134**
ratatouille with pistou **82**
rhubarb
  baked rhubarb and ginger
    cheesecake **108**
  rhubarb and raspberry
    Bakewell slice **128**
rice: nut roast **96**
rose water: white chocolate, rose
  and raspberry blondies **134**

S

salmon: smoked salmon and
  watercress quiche **60**
sausages
  pork, apple and sage pies **59**
  sausage and fennel-seed
    pasta **99**
  sticky sausages and polenta
    chips **87**
scones
  cheese, bacon and chive
    scones **49**
  pumpkin pie scones **145**
shortbread, lavender **137**
spinach
  Brussels sprout, bacon
    and chestnut salad **43**
  lentil and green bean salad
    with ginger dressing **34**
  sausage and fennel-seed
    pasta **99**
  sweet potato and cauliflower
    curry pies **78**
  Thai-style green curry
    soup **16**
  Tuscan-style tomato soup **19**
squash
  beef, ale and horseradish
    cobbler **102**

chicken, leek and tarragon
  pie **85**
honey-roast squash, pearl
  barley and kale **90–1**
squash, feta and sage
  filo bake **62**
strawberries
  lavender and honey
    panna cotta **113**
  summer berry tart **114**
swede
  game and celeriac stew **97**
  lamb hotpot **76**
sweet potatoes
  roasted beetroot, kale
    and Brie quiche **65**
  roasted vegetable soup
    with apple slices **28**
  spiced cauliflower and
    potato parcels **61**
  sweet potato and cauliflower
    curry pies **78**

T

tabbouleh: goat's cheese
  and tabbouleh salad **33**
tarts
  custard tarts **122**
  pea, broccoli and rocket
    tart **52**
  peach frangipane tart **111**
  pear, walnut and Stilton
    quiches **69**
  roasted beetroot, kale
    and Brie quiche **65**
  smoked salmon and
    watercress quiche **60**
  summer berry tart **114**
  summer veg filo tarts **56**
tea-soaked fruit cake **149**
Thai-style green curry soup **16**
tomatoes
  beef, ale and horseradish
    cobbler **102**
  chilli non carne **95**
  goat's cheese and tabbouleh
    salad **33**

hunter's chicken **80**
Moroccan-style chicken
  stew **81**
ratatouille with pistou **82**
summer veg filo tarts **56**
sweet potato and cauliflower
  curry pies **78**
Tuscan-style tomato
  soup **19**

V

vegetables *see also specific
  vegetables*
  roasted vegetable soup
    with apple slices **28**
  spring vegetable pasta
    alfredo **75**
  summer veg filo tarts **56**

W

walnuts
  honey-roast squash, pearl
    barley and kale **90–1**
  pear, walnut and Stilton
    quiches **69**
  roasted beetroot with
    walnuts and Stilton **45**
watercress: smoked salmon
  and watercress quiche **60**
wild garlic soup **14**

Y

yogurt
  baked rhubarb and ginger
    cheesecake **108**
  chicken souvlaki with
    tzatziki **84**
  flatbreads **101**
  roasted aubergine with
    chickpea salad and chilli
    caramelised nuts **40**
  roasted beetroot, kale
    and Brie quiche **65**
  slow-roast spiced shoulder of
    lamb **101**
  spiced cauliflower and potato
    parcels **61**
  summer berry tart **114**